T0199219

Not My Spine

THE UNTOLD STORY
OF THE CAUSE AND COST

ESOSA RUTH IKOLO

authorHOUSE®

AuthorHouse™
1663 Liberty Drive
Bloomington, IN 47403
www.authorhouse.com
Phone: 1 (800) 839-8640

British Library Cataloguing in Publication Data. A catalogue
record for this book is available from the British Library.

Published by AuthorHouse   09/23/2015

ISBN: 978-1-5049-2760-4 (sc)
ISBN: 978-1-5049-2759-8 (e)

Library of Congress Control Number: 2015912605

Print information available on the last page.

Author's Note/Disclaimer

To write this book, I relied on my pregnancy diary and researched facts as contained in online medical databases and websites; all references cited therein have been listed at the end. I also conferred with my consultants as mentioned in the book, and I called upon my own memory of the events which took place during this time of my life. Notes from my medical records played a great part in the writing of this memoir.

Additionally, with the help of family and friends who were present during my ordeal, I have been able to recount more of what happened to me during this period. I have deliberately omitted names where I did not see the need to mention them and obtained permission to use all others.

Most of the dialogue used in this book has been reconstructed from my memory of conversations held years ago.

Acknowledgment

To say the least, I thank God for the opportunity of being a mother. I am profoundly grateful for the gift of life and for healing to my mind and body.

To my dear mother, who is a brilliant writer in her own right and from whom I learnt the very first thing about book writing: your regular reminders that I needed to write my first book motivated me.

To Edwin, my dear husband, for your support: you literally had a day and night job of being daddy, mummy and nanny to JD and me. God bless and repay you. Thanks also for putting up with me during those initial long hours spent writing this book, when I disturbed you with the sounds from the keyboard.

A deep bow to my sons: it's an honour and privilege to be your mother. How can I not dedicate this book specifically to Jedidiah, who is the centre of this story? You are such a caring boy who always asked me about how much progress I was making with this book. You even insisted that I include your picture and that of your brother. And to Jonathan, you are a testament of God's healing of my back. I love you both very much.

To my sweet siblings, Noma, Tracy, Ella, Itohan and Innocent: though you all were far away, I felt your love, prayers and support during my ordeal. God bless you. I love you all.

I am indebted to Auntie for making the telephone call that saved my life. God bless you richly!

To Mosun, Ada, Quobo and Charity, Makamba and Dotun: I am also indebted to you all for being good parents to Jedidiah and for giving him a home at different times when I was sick. May God's fullness continuously rest on you. Special thanks to my friend Bose for being like a second mum to JD. May God reward you abundantly for the plentiful love and gifts you showered on him.

To my pastors Calvin and Pauline and the members of Mount Zion Community Church, who played a major role in my recovery: thank you for your labour of love and prayers.

To the ladies who volunteered at Homestart: you are all stars never to be forgotten.

I am deeply grateful to the friends who nurtured and cared for me, most of whom I met for the first time when they offered to help after hearing of my situation, and who now have become my good friends. There are too many to name but know I appreciate you all from the bottom of my heart. I'd like to particularly mention Patience, Omon, Jumai, Mina, Temby, Egnetia, Pastor Marva, Pam, Okei and Omo. I pray that you will have help whenever you need it.

To my good friend Evelyn, I am grateful for your support and advice all through the writing of this book.

A big thank you to my book club members for their constructive criticisms about this book.

Thank you, Jasmine, for telling me that if I want to write a book, I should *just start* and not procrastinate. This particular piece of advice actually got me writing this book and for this I am grateful!

Dedication

I dedicate this book, my story, to my inestimable friend Esemoni, who passed on to glory in 2012. I miss you dearly and can't stop crying when thinking about the fantastic times we had. Rest in peace my sister, for I know you are in a far better place. I pray for God's profound love and protection to endlessly embrace your children you left behind.

Prologue

There is no greater agony than bearing an untold story inside you. ~ Dr Maya Angelou

I dream and quite a lot. Many months before my baby was conceived, I had a number of dreams in which I saw what he looked like. I also could tell what his sex would be and, to an extent, what his life would bring about. These dreams, plus my own wishes of how I'd be a great mother and do so many things with my baby from the moment he was born, assured me that things were going to be just fine. So I did not have the slightest reason to doubt that I'd have an easy and stress-free pregnancy, nor was I prepared for the major setback pregnancy would bring—a setback that had the potential to paralyse not just my dreams of being a mother, but also to paralyse my body forever.

One thing I am good at is having my picture taken. What joy I derive from looking at photographs and how many hours I could spend going through my collection and reliving the moments captured in each picture. I am looking at one now; it was taken several months after I had my first son, and in it, I am standing opposite the door of our corridor-shaped kitchen, looking in the direction of our living room, in our lakeside flat in Erdington, Birmingham.

In Africa, women nurse their babies in different ways, and one unique way is to wear babies on their back in a cloth wrapped around the mother's torso. To do this, they literally swing the baby from their waist round to the back and secure them with a piece of rectangular cloth known as a wrapper. Tiny babies only a few days old can be wrapped this way and carried until they are two, although it depends on the child's weight. This custom is known to help mothers pacify their babies, providing them with some respite to get on with their chores, while others believe it helps strengthen the back. It is also widely believed that it provides a good physical bond between mother and baby.

If there was one thing I had dreamt of doing when I had my first baby, it was this, so looking at this picture of me with my baby tied to my back brings joyful tears. I definitely wasn't doing it with the idea of strengthening my back; instead, I was determined to have my baby on my back, no matter the cost. I cry as I recall the physical, mental and emotional torture I went through during the second and third trimesters of my pregnancy.

Still looking at this picture, I reminisce about the times when I'd look at my days-old baby as he lay innocently on the bed next to me. I would be scared of touching him for fear that I might drop him due to the debilitating pain I was under, caused by what I later learned to be a collapsed spine. A certain mycobacterium had been living in my body for a good while and had, unknown to me, severely infected my spine. This disease was not common then but is now increasing—not only in developing countries, but also in developed nations—affecting both young and old. It is a disease with far-reaching effects on the victim, having the potential to render them paralysed and completely helpless. I am saddened, realising that neither I nor my doctors were able to detect this illness when it initially presented in the way it did, and even though my doctors were quite limited in their ability to diagnose and treat me due to my pregnancy, I remain totally puzzled at their level of inattentiveness to my situation post-childbirth.

After childbirth, I underwent a major surgical operation that kept me apart from my few-weeks-old baby. I was strongly warned by my neurosurgeon not to put much strain on my back, which had a long road of recovery ahead. So while I look at this picture, feeling like I had achieved my age-long dream, one could also say I went against my doctor's orders: I had my baby, nine months old and weighing around ten kilos, on my back. I had him there for no more than a couple of minutes, after I succeeded in cajoling my husband into taking the picture as a keepsake.

I struggled for a long time to come to terms with being infected with the disease, mainly because of my lack of adequate knowledge about it and the stigma I believed was associated with it. For a long time, I was in the dark and refused to embrace the truth about what had caused my illness and so was unable to tell anyone about its true cause, even those who helped me when I was sick. Thus, it was no easy task for me to decide to put down on paper my recollection of what happened.

I share this with the expectation that a life, and perhaps more, will be spared the dire cost I had to pay. I hope you will be inspired by my story and, most importantly, learn about what made me sick and how to watch out for its grave symptoms. Also, through my experience, it is hoped that people will learn to dig deep and ask for second, third and fourth opinions, if need be, about their illnesses and not give up after just one, for life is precious and must not be toyed with.

Chapter 1

It was a small wedding but one with such lovely memories. Edwin and I married in July 2007.

"I sense strongly that by the same time next year you will be pregnant," Edwin said to me on the night of our wedding.

I lay next to him trying to absorb this intriguing piece of information. If I am honest, I did not think much of this statement at the time and also did not attempt to ask more about his certainty of it. I believe that as a new bride, I must have smiled quite shyly and responded with a resounding amen.

A couple of weeks after our wedding, I returned to England from Nigeria to start a new civil engineering graduate job while Edwin attended to other important things, including beginning the application for his spousal visa so he could join me.

On the 17th of December 2007, I travelled on the National Express coach to meet Edwin at Heathrow Airport, and we took the same coach back to the house I shared with three other people in the Sutton Coldfield area of Birmingham. Despite the fact that he was carsick for most of the journey, I felt really excited about my new life with him, and in order to give him a good first-time welcome to England, I had asked for three weeks leave off work. Usually when people take that amount of time off work, they have made great plans to engage in some fun trip or activity, but I had not; all I knew was I was going to spend time with my husband, and it did not matter how or where.

Barely two weeks after my husband joined me in the UK, I became pregnant with our first child. I can still clearly picture the night I secretly took the home pregnancy test and shared the great news with Edwin who, though not one to show his emotions, was glad too. I went to bed feeling grateful for the gift and thrilled about the months ahead. Bursting with excitement and joy, I recalled the dreams I had prior to getting married and knew that although I had not done the sex scan for the pregnancy, it would be a boy. I also believed this baby would be a blessing and a joy, just as I had been told in one of my dreams.

I was overcome with shyness about telling anyone about it and debated over when I should let my colleagues at work know. I decided to first tell my female office manager and asked her not to tell anyone until the pregnancy showed. Understandably, and perhaps because she was a mother herself, she immediately promised not to tell, although she didn't fail to tease me about my shyness. After telling our families and friends the good news, you can count on the fact that our few friends in England, although happy for us, were surprised at how soon this had happened and teased us about it at every turn.

Dreams have always been a part of me, and by dreams I mean those one has when asleep. Over the years, I have grown to understand that I should not read meaning into all my dreams; however, I also recognise that some do have deep meanings, and those I do not ignore.

Thirty-one weeks into my pregnancy, I had such a dream. In this dream, I had attended a Christian outreach or crusade and carried my baby boy in his pushchair while I looked for Edwin, who seemed to be lost in the crowd. Out of the blue, I heard a prayer come from a tiny but powerful voice and looked around for the source. To my utter shock it came from my baby in his pushchair! I can clearly recall some of the words, including 'all men will see the glory of God and give him thanks'. I woke up from the dream and was filled with both trepidation and joy, because to me this was a dream with a message. Little did I know that through these dreams I was being prepared for a challenging time ahead and, though unknown to me then, also being assured of God's sovereign power and protection.

My twelve-week scan was done in March. Edwin and I attended our appointment at Good Hope Hospital in Sutton Coldfield. As the sonographer ran the transducer on my tummy, I could see the baby's image and little movements on the screen. As I listened to my baby's heartbeat, tears rolled down my face, and I silently thanked God for blessing me with this gift which I did not feel I deserved. Even though Edwin did not fully understand why I was crying, he comforted me. On that day, we were dead broke; I was the only one working at the time and payday was days away, but as God would have it, the midwife who took the sonogram pictures did not charge us a dime. I clung to that picture dearly and for a long time gazed at it often, as if trying to see if the image resembled the face of the baby in my dreams.

I would imagine what my baby's face looked like, and this made me look forward even more to the day I would give birth to him. I was keen to understand what pregnancy and motherhood entailed and so, together with the knowledge from my antenatal classes, I read as much as I could. One book, *Supernatural Childbirth* by Jackie Mize, was given to me by a friend. It is a story about how a pregnant woman experiences supernatural victory in her pregnancy and childbirth through her strong faith. As the pregnancy progressed, I continued to ponder the little gift inside me and as a Christian, I studied the Bible and prayed over God's promises to my unborn baby, hoping I would experience an equally amazing childbirth.

I had my scheduled twenty-week scan in May, which was when the sex of the baby would be determined. Unfortunately, my baby was not lying in a position that aided easy identification of his male genitals, if it were to be a boy, so I was asked to return after two weeks. By this time, I had begun to suffer from Pregnancy-related Pelvic Girdle Pain (PPGP)—a condition resulting in stiffness of the pelvic joints causing medium to severe pain which makes moving around difficult. I also began to experience intermittent chest pain and occasional back pain, all of which I put down to being pregnant; according to the stories I'd heard, pregnancy comes with all sorts of symptoms.

I eventually had my scan and was told my baby's sex. As Edwin was unable to attend this appointment with me due to a job interview, I decided not to tell him the truth about the baby's gender.

"How did it go today at the hospital? Did they tell you the baby's sex?" Edwin asked after he got back home later that day.

"I was told we are having a girl," I replied.

The moment I said that, my tummy made a funny noise which, according to Edwin, was a definite sign that I was lying—which, of course, I was.

One other thing I did at an early stage of my pregnancy was to draw up a list of my preferred baby names, and so one day I told Edwin of my top pick for the first time: Daniel. I explained my reasons for choosing the name Daniel, which is a biblical name with qualities that symbolised everything I desired in our son, but Edwin had a different take and told me he already had a name. I felt a little annoyed about this, because there I was gloating about what I felt was a unique name for our child, not knowing he already had a name selected—and his decision was final.

"Shouldn't we have discussed our choices together before settling on a name for our baby?" I muttered, though I could see from his countenance it was a lost fight.

Up until this point, Edwin had been unsuccessfully job hunting. It was a low time for us because we did not have enough money, but like every expectant mother, I had my drawn-up list of baby things which we simply could not afford on our meagre income. Three months before my due date we still did not have one tangible item for our baby. I had read about a charity event called Nearly New Sale, where people sold off their old and unwanted baby things, so I decided to attend the next event. With little money in my purse, I was fortunate to get some nice baby items and went home with a smile.

Though he had a couple of work stints now and again, Edwin continued to struggle to find a decent job. There had been one stint he had for five days, helping a woman sell her goods at the National Exhibition Centre. Then he got a marketing job, which made him quite happy. With this he was full of high hopes, believing that once he understood the tricks of the trade and pitched well to his customers, money would begin to flow in.

I personally did not like marketing jobs, because they usually had a catch to them and involved too much stress just to sell a product. For people who are born marketers—if there are such people—it's a piece of cake; for others like me who struggle with being told no when selling anything, it is frustrating! Anyway, I was grateful Edwin finally had a job and no longer had to sit at home looking miserable. He carried on quite well with it and was very keen, looking forward to spending his first salary on me and our unborn baby.

As a naturally private man, one would hardly know when Edwin was worried unless it was quite serious. One night he came home after doing his door-to-door rounds of pitching to potential customers and told me he had knocked on one door only to be threatened rudely by the homeowner, who promised to send his dog at him if he did not leave immediately. I sympathised with him and encouraged him, even though I knew this sort of job did not suit his personality, just as it did not suit mine.

One cold winter night about a month into the job, he came home and took off his rain-soaked shoes.

"I have quit the job," Edwin blurted.

I pretended not to have heard him, as surely this could not have been the same job he'd been certain would bring in so much money and make his dreams—our dreams— come true.

"Sorry, I did not hear what you just said. Could you say that again?" I said.

When he repeated himself, I rejoiced inside! Regardless of our desperate need for money, I couldn't have been happier about this news. We both continued to believe God would provide a better job that did not require so much stress and harassment.

Weeks passed into months and still Edwin had no job. This became a fast-growing concern for us given I was only a few months from the start of my maternity leave. I was also conscious that my salary, which was just about sufficient for both of us, would reduce soon after the government's statutory maternity pay kicked in post-childbirth. And with the unpleasant pains I was having, I could no longer cope with this additional problem. After a long and hard think, I came up with a plan—or so I thought.

Next to my former office is a church. I decided that during my lunchtime hour, I would go in there and pray about this challenge. To do this, I was off food for the first half of each day as I carried out a time of fasting and praying. One day, after I had been doing this for about three days, an older lady who had seen me praying with my tear-stained eyes came to me.

"Are you all right?" the lady asked. "If you need us to pray for you, you could write your prayer request and leave it there." She pointed towards the altar. I thanked her for the kind gesture but continued praying.

By the end of that week, Edwin got a job offer and was asked to start work at the end of July. To say I was glad would be a gross understatement, for after six months, my husband had finally landed a decent job with one of the city banks, which meant that we would be able to afford a decent life for our baby. I was on cloud nine!

Chapter 2

Birds had largely stopped singing and the berries were beginning to ripen. The peak of British summertime was gradually creeping in, even though it did not feel like it with parts of the country, including Birmingham, experiencing heavy rainfall.

It was late June and although I had hoped that the pains I was having in my chest, back and pelvis would have eased off, they increased significantly, limiting the number of things I could easily do. I dreaded coughing and sneezing, to the point that I tried to guesstimate when I needed to do so in order to come up with some counter action to subdue it. Also, I was often out of breath. There were times when I went out with friends and prayed that there would be no speed bumps on the roads, as they caused me a lot of pain when the car went over them. Because of this, if I remembered beforehand, I would plead with the person driving to change routes so as to avoid moaning whenever that moment came.

Having PPGP was a nightmare; it had begun to greatly affect my mobility. Getting up after sitting for a while was painful and as we did not have a car, our main means of transportation was the bus. Alighting at our destination was always dreadful. Oftentimes my dear husband would plead with me to prepare for the 'big activity' by getting up as early as two bus stops before the one we needed, just so it would save us time and the embarrassment of people looking at us when I eventually stood up, discomfort written all over my face, and waddled my way out of the bus.

One day while at work, I felt a strangely sharp pain in my chest that went round my back like a ring, making me stop dead in my tracks. It was excruciating; I could hardly move and a colleague kindly offered to drive me to the nearest hospital, which was Good Hope Hospital. A few checks were done and the pregnancy was monitored for a while, but it did not reveal anything. I asked for a chest x-ray, but due to the pregnancy this was immediately refused. After some hours, the pains subsided a bit and I was sent home.

I continued to be racked with these pains, the worst of which were in my chest and back. Though I wished it would go away, I did not worry much about the back pains because I'd read it is a characteristic of pregnancy, given the baby's weight places strain on the spine. It was the stubborn pain in my chest I could do without because breathing was becoming very difficult; I feared I was going to die.

It was the first Saturday in August and, out of nowhere, Edwin suggested we go out to the city centre.

"What for?" I asked him, looking quite quizzical.

"Oh, it's just to take your mind off the pains," Edwin replied.

I was not satisfied by this answer but thought it was indeed a good idea to be out for a change, and as Edwin is an introvert, I felt I should avail myself of this golden opportunity to go out with him. After walking aimlessly around the city centre for what felt like hours, Edwin suggested we go into Birmingham Museum and Art Gallery. This was the first time I'd gone into this place; as a matter of fact, I did not realise it existed even though I'd been that way a few times.

Whilst having a look at some of the beautiful displays of artwork and masterpieces, I noticed Edwin did not seem as interested as he should be, given he brought me there in the first place. He was constantly on his phone.

"Who are you chatting with?" I asked him, feeling piqued by this behaviour. "I could have stayed back in bed, you know, if this is what you prefer doing." I was fuming!

"It is no one," Edwin said. "I think it's time for us to go home."

On our way home, I did not say a word to him and getting home, I went straightaway to our bedroom to rest my sore back. Shortly after, Edwin came in and asked if I wanted a drink. I nodded expecting him to walk away and get me the drink; instead, he stood by the room door gazing at me.

"What is it? Where is the drink?" I asked. What he said next surprised me.

"Why don't you go get it yourself?" Edwin retorted.

At this point, I truly thought he had either lost his mind or he was winding me up for a reason I was not ready to entertain, so I ignored him. He walked away and came back like a man on a mission, trying to convince me about why I needed to go to the kitchen myself.

"It is better if you go get the drink yourself, you know," said Edwin.

"Okay, I have had enough. I really don't need a drink but just want to sleep," I said.

This man would not take no. So to get him off my back, I stood up and slightly pushed him out of my way as I took five steps from my bedroom to the living room door to quickly get the drink and have a most deserved respite. As soon as I opened the door, I heard screams and shouts of "surprise!" from the eight ladies and their young kids who were gathered in our living room. This was too much of a shock to me and I slumped to the floor. Thankfully, I recovered quickly and realised that all the while, unknown to me, Edwin and my female friends had been planning a baby shower party for me. There was lots of food, drinks and also gifts for our unborn baby. No wonder he acted weird, wanting to take me out of the house when he knew how much pain I was suffering from and pretending he had the least interest for the arts by taking me to the gallery. He had successfully planned this with my friends over the past weeks and tactically took me out of the house to give them the opportunity to decorate the living room with baby things and prepare some light food. Even though he was a poor actor, I was grateful to him and, of course, my dear friends for this very lovely gesture.

Going to Good Hope Hospital soon became a regular occurrence whenever I felt really ill or when the pains became unbearable. As the pains grew, so did the coughing.

In the middle of August I went to the hospital and I saw the consultant gynaecologist who, seeing the state I was in, admitted me immediately. He, who had on different occasions refused to allow me to have any x-ray due to the risk it posed to my unborn child, this time (though quite reluctantly) agreed that I have a CT scan done. So on the 19th of August, I was taken in a wheelchair to the scan section of the hospital, and a heavy bag of lead was wrapped around my tummy to prevent the rays from harming the baby. Samples of my blood were also taken for a number of tests and the next day I was told that the scan results showed the lymph nodes in my chest region were enlarged and circular.

With this, the doctor was led to believe that I had contracted Tuberculosis (TB).

"Were you given BCG vaccination as a baby?" the doctor asked as he tried to understand why my lymph nodes looked that way.

"Yes," I answered, showing him the scar on my upper left arm to prove it.

My due date was not until the 8th of September, but the doctor said that if I had indeed contracted TB, I would have to be induced and delivered of the baby so as not to put the baby in further danger. Regardless of their belief of me having TB, Edwin and I dismissed the idea not believing it. We were vindicated in our stance when the sputum test came back negative. I was also told the scan showed my chest was clear. So I was indeed free of TB! A few days later I got discharged but by the evening of the next day I was back in the ward because of the growing chest and back pains which lasted longer and further impeded my breathing.

After the scan results came, not much was said about whether the enlarged lymph nodes were linked to my pains, other than that a procedure known as an endoscopy—the insertion of an instrument down my throat in order to see what was happening in my chest would be done after I had the baby. The doctor also said that as Good Hope Hospital did not offer that service, I would be given an appointment in a different hospital in Birmingham. For the sake of my baby, I was determined to wait it out and hoped I would survive till then.

As I grew impatient about my condition, so did my gynaecologist who was forced to say that he might have to carry out a Caesarean section (C-section) on me because he did not think I would be able to withstand the rigors of labour. By this time I was struggling to walk or even sit upright and though I could understand his concerns, I remember saying "No doctor, I am not having a C-section!"

I fully understood my doctor's concerns, but I also held on to my belief that God would give me that which I had asked for, which was to have a safe and natural childbirth. I am quite sure my doctor, who was only trying to help me, must have looked at me and thought I was simply ignorant of the scale of my problems. Maybe I was.

Following this, my doctor opted for an induced labour on the 29th of August 2008, and so at about 9 p.m. on that day I was induced by the midwife. Labour was a heck of an experience. With the aid of gas and an air mouthpiece, it was quite bearable. As it progressed, however, I did not have the strength in my legs to push during contractions. I asked Edwin, who stood by my bedside comforting me, to hold my legs apart while I concentrated on pushing rather than on my weak legs, but the midwife did not let him. With the pains from labour and my back killing me, my resolve not to have any artificial pain relief went out of the window. I heard myself scream out, "Get me an epidural, please!" By the time the anaesthetist arrived and prepared his gadgets, our dear son was born; it was 9.27 a.m. on Saturday morning. We named him Jedidiah. He looked beautiful, with really long legs. How I managed to push out a baby in spite of the agonizing pains I was having, I do not know. Instead of rejoicing at the birth of my baby, I was glad I would soon begin to feel well, either naturally or from the treatment I was certain to receive following the diagnosis from the endoscopy procedure I had been promised.

My gynaecologist, who was absent during the actual birth, came round the ward a couple of days later and congratulated me for my bravery and determination to deliver naturally, even against the odds. Before he left, I was quick to ask about the endoscopy and he assured me he was making the required arrangements. The next day there was still no sign of this forthcoming. I became very anxious and instead of concentrating on my new baby, I continued to be overwhelmed by the pains in my back which seemed to have increased tenfold, worsening my ability to carry out a number of actions. When bending over and moving around it felt like a blade was piercing my side; breathing was now heavier and more difficult, making me all the more miserable. I struggled to pick up my baby from the bed and breastfeeding him caused me a lot of pain.

A few times when I was with Edwin or with friends who visited, I would cry out in despair.

"Why me? Why do I have to suffer this way?"

All they could really do was offer words of comfort, telling me everything would be all right. Edwin and I were very confused; we were in a place where we ought to get expert medical advice and help but none was being rendered. We didn't know what to do or where else to turn but we continued to hope against hope that help would come. With our son now with us, we tried to look on the bright side.

Right after giving birth, I was treated kindly by the hospital staff; the nurses on duty even offered to look after my baby for a few hours from time to time to allow me to catch some rest. Also, as I was still weak and in a lot of pain, they usually brought my meals to the room that I alone occupied with my baby. This help was such a huge relief given that walking was not my favourite thing; considering how long it took for me to clean my baby and myself, I was grateful for this gesture.

One morning, after waiting to be served breakfast at the usual time, it did not come so I decided to find out why it was delayed. After I pressed the call bell, a nurse came and upon listening to the reason for my call, she said, "You have to walk to the kitchen yourself because we will no longer be able to bring you food."

Astonished by these words and as it was now past breakfast time, I told her I was ravenous and pleaded with her to find me some food. She then advised me to go check the kitchen for any leftovers. I will never forget the walk to that kitchen! I thought it would never end.

By day four post-delivery, I pushed again to see my gynaecologist to learn what progress he had made with the appointment.

"I have not been successful with getting you the appointment," my gynaecologist said apologetically.

I truly did not know what to make of this. "But I thought my pregnancy was the only thing stopping you from doing what had to be done," I said, my voice filled with weary sadness.

"Yes, and I have made efforts to contact the relevant people but given I don't pay their salaries, I can't do anything more than I have already done, I'm afraid."

Now that the baby was out I just could not comprehend why things weren't happening as fast as they should. If the test result showed that my lymph nodes were enlarged, which from every indication did not seem like a normal thing, I expected I would be whisked off right after delivery to undergo a series of additional tests or x-rays, but this was not the case. At that point I regretted terribly that back in Nigeria I did not make enough credits in my Secondary School Certificate Examination to study my dream course, medicine, because if I had, I would have been more in tune with what was happening to me and perhaps might have known what ought to be done.

Anyone who saw me could easily tell that something was wrong, but after some days in the delivery ward, my doctor felt confident to sign my discharge papers. I was told that I would be going home on the 4th of September on the basis that I was medically stable. I pleaded with them to let me stay and even my mother in Nigeria, upon hearing my plight, advised that I should stay and get all the help I could get in hospital; she could tell from afar that I was not well enough to be discharged.

"Please let me stay a few more days," I said to the nurse on duty as she came to do her last routine check on me.

"I am only obeying orders" she said.

"If you can keep me in hospital for five days after childbirth, what harm could a few more days do?"

I was hopeful that if they kept me back, some new symptoms would spring up which could aid their diagnosis, but no one was listening.

Of course I was keen to go home with my much-dreamt-about son in my arms. I was eager to be a proper mum to him and, to state the obvious, he needed to go to the home that had been so lovingly prepared for his arrival. I had greatly missed my homemade spicy and tasty foods, so surely home was the place to be, but I knew that if I went home in my current state I would be useless to him. I could not take care of myself, so how in the world I was expected to care for a delicate baby of just a few days old I couldn't comprehend!

Come the 4th of September, Edwin arrived after work to take us home. Before we set out he talked with the staff one more time to try to convince them to keep me back, but to no avail. At 6 p.m. we were nicely escorted outside the reception of the Fothergill maternity unit of the hospital, where our friend Patience, awaited to drive us home.

"You never know, you may even feel better when you get home," one of the nurses said as they bade us farewell.

Weary and in pain, I had no response to offer.

Chapter 3

On arrival at the parking lot of our block of flats, Edwin took our baby upstairs to our flat while I asked Patience to drive her car closer to the building so as to shorten my walk. I struggled but eventually managed to get out of the car and was glad I could actually take small steps. I must have rejoiced too soon for after only a few steps I felt a sharp stabbing pain in my chest that sent me right down the ground. All I could do was to cry out for help. Luckily, there were some young lads playing football in the fields nearby who, when they heard my cry, ran to me.

"My flat number is 6. Call my husband, please," I managed to mumble to the boys who immediately ran off and got Edwin. Edwin helped me to our bed where I lay all evening and into the night. Unfortunately, the seizure happened again in the middle of the night and it scared the life out of me, leaving me wondering if this was going to be a regular occurrence.

It was, therefore, no surprise that at the crack of dawn we were at our local general practitioner's (GP) surgery. We explained all that had happened from the birth of our baby to last night's event. We also told him of the pending specialist appointment in Selly Oak Hospital, which my gynaecologist had said would be the place for the endoscopy. After listening to us, my GP who also could not tell the cause of my ill health rang Good Hope Hospital to inquire about the referral, but when he did not succeed in speaking with anyone, he advised us that the best thing to do was to show up at any Accident and Emergency (A & E) unit where he was sure we would get the necessary medical attention. We did not do as the GP advised; why would we? I had already been in a medical facility where I ought to have been listened to and kept under strict supervision, but no one cared. Surely we had by now lost faith in referrals and doctors perceptions of what was wrong with me. All we wanted was a quick solution to my problem and as this was not forthcoming, we went back home and hoped to God for a miracle.

Perhaps we could have handled the situation differently had I not been so ill but we were unable to think things through. I had lived in England for nearly five years up until this time but I was relatively new in Birmingham. Edwin had only been in the country for nine months and had never really had a need for medical attention until my case, so he did not fully understand how things worked. Aside from a handful of friends and a few church members with whom we were somewhat acquainted, we had no family members in England who could be there for us in every sense of the word. We were on our own.

I needed help with looking after the baby, to say the least, and it suddenly dawned on me that we had been so consumed by my deteriorating health that we had forgotten to apply for a visitor's visa for my mum. The last time she'd visited me was in 2004, in Newcastle upon Tyne where I studied for a master's degree, and although I had seen her in 2007 when I travelled home for my wedding, there was no better time to see her again. I recalled one time we talked on phone during the early days of my pregnancy and I told her she would stay in the small 'box' room we had in our two-bedroom flat, but the one important thing needed to bring her here had been forgotten. It was only now, after being discharged from Good Hope Hospital, that we remembered to ask her to make the application.

Only a month into his new job, Edwin was not entitled to paternity leave but his kind-hearted boss gave him a week off work from the day our baby was born. Sadly, this leave was coming to an end and the thought of being left alone to care for our baby made me panic.

Edwin did his best to make sure everything was within my reach before leaving home that Monday morning. "Everything will be fine! Don't fear, God will be with you," he said reassuringly before leaving for work.

Luckily Jedidiah whom we also refer to as JD, was on only breast milk so there was no need for Edwin to prepare bottle feeds for him but shortly after he left I had my first challenge. I needed to change my baby's nappy and the pains, which had naturally intensified, stopped me from lifting my head or doing anything. I was also breathing heavily and if I was ever concerned for my baby's well-being, this was the one time to be. I was terrified I would drop him on the floor or die of the pain and cannot tell how I managed to take care of him that whole day and even the week after. Edwin of course helped only in the evenings and weekends as did a few friends who visited sometimes, but none were available during the day when I really needed more help.

Though not mandatory, it is part of the African culture to officially name a baby on the eighth day after birth, as we believe that by this time the baby is quite strong and ready to be shown to people. And as we had been forcefully sent home from hospital, we felt it was worth having this important event which is also a time of celebration when family and friends come together to fellowship, pray and dine. So our son's naming ceremony was fixed for Saturday the 6th of September and our few but lovely friends arranged it all on our behalf. They prepared the food and drinks; all I needed to do was show up on the day in our living room where the guests would be gathered. I spent the whole day preparing to attend this occasion, and by prepare I mean psyching myself to get out of bed and get myself and my baby dressed. I usually struggled to get in and out of bed because of the pain and so on this day, even though I had planned to commence getting ready well ahead of the event start time of 5 p.m., I just could not because I felt very ill. Well past 5 p.m. a couple of friends came into my bedroom to see how I was getting on and when they saw I had not made any progress, they helped me out of bed. After much effort and with their assistance, I got dressed and joined the guests who had been waiting for us all this while. Some guests who did not know me well were obviously wondering why I looked the way I did. Thus I was quite glad when our friend, the pastor for the ceremony, began to preach and asked everyone to pray for me to get well quickly so I could be a mother to my baby. The fun continued as guests chatted and dined together while I sneaked back into my safe zone, my bedroom, to lie down.

Given when we had asked my mum to apply for her visa and the time it usually took to get a decision, we knew the earliest she might arrive in England was not until three weeks. So on Monday the 15th of September, after Edwin had gone to work, I knew I had to organise interim help, otherwise either myself or my two-week-old baby would be in great danger. I got out my phone and scrolled through my contact list to see if I could find someone—anyone—I knew who was not at work and would not mind coming round to help. I was glad when I came to the name of the older sister of an old school friend. I had met her twice before and later learned she is the sister-in-law of a friend of my mum; her husband's family and my mother had been friends for a long time back in Nigeria. Aside from this, the lady, whom I call Auntie, had seemed nice when I met her and both reasons gave me the courage to call her that Monday morning. As she was not aware that I'd had my baby, I started the conversation with the good news.

"Auntie, baby is here!" I said, and before she could congratulate me, I added, "and I am not well."

In no time, she arrived and was astonished to see the state I was in.

"What is the matter? Why do you look this way?" she asked.

Before I could reply, she asked me to pack a few things for me and baby and took us straight to her house in Smethwick. This was a welcome surprise!

Although an invitation was the last thing on my mind when I made that call, my prompt acceptance to go to auntie's house was a no-brainer and, truth be told, when Edwin got to know about it later, he was glad she could help! Days after we arrived at her house, we got the good news that my mum had been given a two-year visitor's visa. I was ecstatic; it felt like all my problems would now be solved!

My baby and I stayed in Auntie's bedroom for the entire period we were there and she was very kind to us, attending to our every need and preparing any meal I wanted. When we ran out of nappies and before Edwin could come down with a new supply, she would dash to the shops to fetch some. Her sister, who is my friend, visited Birmingham during this time and also helped care for me and my baby. She'd massage my sore back and once while doing so, she said she noticed a sort of bulge or swelling in the middle of my back. As no one understood what this was, we did not think much of it. Another time, she prepared the bath for me to soak myself in and though I got in there unaided, I could not get out by myself, no matter how hard I tried.

Towards the end of my first week at Auntie's house, I started to notice changes in my legs. Walking became quite difficult and I was having twitches at different places on my legs, a condition known as myoclonic jerks. I also had become numb from below my breasts down to my legs; all this happened in the space of a day or two.

Auntie had a friend who came visiting one day. She advised me that due to the pains I was having, it was probably wise for me to get the baby off my breast, especially as I did not know what was causing the pains. I was angry to hear that because breastfeeding was one of the things I had dreamt of doing when I became a mother. I had also promised myself I would breastfeed exclusively for at least six months because experts say it is the best form of food for a baby. So I certainly was not going to entertain anyone, and certainly not a stranger, telling me to desist, even though I must admit she had a point.

Auntie's husband is a medical doctor who at the time was somewhere in Africa working for an international organisation. I believe that as an older mother herself, and with the influence of her husband, she just could not accept that my illness was superficial. First thing on the morning of Sunday the 21st of September, the seventh day of us living in her house, she called an ambulance. When the paramedic arrived, she explained my condition to him and showed him the protrusion in my back.

"Something is definitely not right there," he said as soon as he saw it.

He took me straight to City Hospital A & E while Auntie drove behind us with my baby in her car. Maybe now I would get the answers I so desperately needed.

Chapter 4

On arrival at City Hospital, I was assessed and an x-ray was asked to be done immediately. "Your spine is fractured!" said the lady doctor who examined me. "Did you have a fall or trauma in the past?"

"No . . ." I said, a bit perplexed by her question. Surely if I'd had a fall that was enough to break my spine, I would have known.

This news did not quite hit home as it should have. I took it in gradually, trying not to lose sight of my baby who was asleep in his pushchair next to me in one of the open wards, given Auntie had left to go to church that morning and Edwin was on his way to meet us.

"You need urgent medical attention," the doctor said, and she began to arrange for me to be transferred to Queen Elizabeth Hospital (QE) for specialist help.

Things were now happening quickly and with neither Auntie nor Edwin in sight, I was concerned for my baby.

"Can my baby come with me to the QE?" I asked the doctor.

"Sorry, babies are not allowed into the hospital unit because there are no facilities to cater for them."

I could not believe she was telling me that I will not be allowed to take my three-week-old baby with me. *How on earth did they expect he'd be cared for without me?* I wondered.

"Surely there must be a way to have mother and baby in hospital," I added, unrelenting, as if I had not heard what she had been saying. No matter how much I pleaded and cried, the doctor's answer remained the same. I just could not imagine being away from him and refused to lose sight of him until Edwin eventually showed up.

Given that I was now on statutory maternity pay, we relied mainly on Edwin's income. Being only a few weeks into his new job, he could not afford to take additional time off work. So, taking JD home that night would have been difficult because Edwin had to go to work the next day. At that point I wished we were financially buoyant, with all the money in the world, so Edwin would not have to work but could just be a father and mother to our son. If wishes were horses, beggars would ride on them indeed!

When Auntie returned, she kindly agreed to take JD back to her house while I was prepared to be taken to the QE that night. Before they left me, I kissed my dear baby and we said our goodbyes, not realising what lay ahead. We arrived at the QE at past midnight and on getting there, the paramedics used a flat, rigid board known as a slide board to move me from the stretcher to a hospital bed. I soon got used to being on these boards at subsequent times when I was routinely taken for scans and x-rays within the hospital; I found them quite good and safe in transferring patients with back problems, preventing falls and providing some assurance to both the patient and the people using them.

While at the QE, I explained my symptoms to the doctor on duty and told him of the ongoing pains on the left side of my chest and in my back. I told him how heavy and numb my legs had become. After taking down notes he assessed me further, conducting sensory and reflex examinations on my legs with use of dull needles and a hammer. After this he asked me to lift my legs and wriggle my toes, both of which I struggled to do. A full blood test was done and I was booked for an urgent MRI scan later that day. The MRI scan was done with the focus on my entire trunk and, when I got into that large scan chamber—which I later became much more familiar with than I liked—I prayed to God to save my life and hoped I would come out in one piece at the other end. The scan revealed that four of my vertebrae had collapsed and this was causing a build-up of pus on both sides of my spinal cord.

The scan also showed that my spinal cord was compressed and this, as I was made to understand, meant my spine was in great danger. The only remedy was for them to conduct emergency surgery on it the same day. In contrast to my time at Good Hope Hospital, I now became used to things being done at a fast pace. After the scan results, I hardly was given any time to think things through and was told that any delay could be detrimental to my body.

From his accent and name I could tell that the consultant who came to give me the surgery briefing and the consent form to sign was a Nigerian and so I used this opportunity to ask him some throbbing questions, hoping that as my fellow African brother, as we normally say, he'd give me a truer account of what was going on. After he finished speaking and with my baby still on my mind, having been separated from him for a day, I felt I still had a fighting chance of bringing him to live with me in hospital.

"Doctor, please can my baby come live with me here?"

Again I was told it was not possible.

"Ok but please tell me, how bad would you say my situation is?" I asked. "Can I not have medicine instead of surgery?"

"No, Mrs Ikolo, your situation is critical and if I were in your shoes, I would agree to surgery," said the consultant.

I had breastfed my baby up until the morning before and missed him dearly. I missed him more when I looked at my hospital gown and saw how soaked it was with milk from my full and heavy breasts. The more I looked down at my gown the more it made me cry and long for my baby to be with me. Later on in hospital, I continued to lactate and my breasts hurt me so much that it got to the point that the matron had to request a midwife from the neighbouring hospital (Birmingham Women's Hospital) to come examine me to see if she could stop the milk flow. The midwife came and said I had the option of letting it dry up naturally or taking a medication to stop the flow. Even though I had consented to her coming over, I refused the latter option because I felt I still stood a chance of breastfeeding my son after I was discharged, so I did not want the flow to cease. I thought about his sounds, his smiles, and how someone else instead of me was looking after him. Oh, those were the worst days of my life and I could not help but feel despondent and responsible for my predicament. *Why me, God?* I wondered as I struggled to come to terms with all that was happening to me. I asked God many questions, crying out to Him in my pain and confusion.

Edwin got to the hospital after work that night and as I had still not fully comprehended the scale of what was happening to me, I quizzed him as if to get him to refuse surgery on my behalf. He said if surgery was the only way out, then we should go for it. So, consent form signed, I was wheeled to the preparatory room and after a three-hour period, the surgery was complete. I woke up in the recovery room and was told it had been a success. While I was being told the good news about the surgery, I wondered why Edwin had not yet told me that my mum was in town. But instead, I got a phone call; it was my mum calling from Nigeria!

From my late teenage years right up to when I was at university in Nigeria, I suffered from an illness characterised by aches and pains in my bones, nausea, lack of appetite and weakness, heavy head and breathlessness. From the time I first noticed this to years afterwards, my mum took me to different doctors, hoping for the illness to be diagnosed. When after several visits they could not come up with an answer, my family and I were left with accepting and living with it. It was quite odd and funny at the same time because even though I felt ill, anyone looking at me could not tell I was unwell. However, if they lived closely with me like my family did, they would have been able to understand why there was usually a lot of fuss around me when I was going through these episodes. The only way I could cope with the illness when I had such spells was to lie in bed for as long as

I could until I had a bit of respite and could carry on with my life as normal.

It was a place I hated being and I know my mother, who was perpetually concerned, would have sold her life to have me feel well, if that were possible. After I graduated from university, I worked in the country's capital city of Abuja and during that time I had a bout of this illness. Living in a place that was a six-hour car ride from home meant I had no ready support or help from family. Having suffered alone for a few days, I thought to inform my mum. In an exhausted and sick state, I sent her a text which was either sent incomplete or, due to a network issue, only delivered half the intended message because all she received was the first part:

Hello Mummy, I am not well at all and if I do not feel better by morning...

The next morning I was woken up by a knock on the door of my rented flat, and who was there before me? My mother.

"Mummy!" I exclaimed.

"So-oo nwam (Esosa my child)!" said my mum. "How are you? When I read your message I became very worried not knowing what you'd do as a result."

My dear mother became overly worried upon reading my half-delivered text message and she asked her driver to take her on an ad hoc long distance trip from Asaba in the south to Abuja in the middle of Nigeria. She abandoned everything, including my little sister who was at secondary school and her day job as a Director in the Ministry of Education.

This was how my hardworking and God-fearing mother was there for my siblings and me—she did not take our matters lightly at all.

So when instead of seeing her I heard her voice on the other end of the phone, I suspected something was wrong. *Surely she was still coming to England,* I thought. The last time I had spoken with her, a couple of days ago, she had made plans to purchase a return flight ticket, so I knew money was not the problem. Also, one of my sisters told me that before she left home for university she had personally packed my mum's bags, ready for her to make her way to Lagos the next day, from where she was to fly to England.

With these thoughts racing through my mind, I anxiously listened for her next words, which seemed to take a long time to come, as though she did not know the best way to tell me what she had to say. Eventually, she let it out between sobs.

"So-oo nwam, I got an instruction from God not to come over and I am so sorry, my daughter," said my mum. With some hesitation she continued talking. "I have known for a few days but did not know how to react let alone tell you about it."

Although in a lot of pain from the very fresh surgery, I made an attempt to sit up just so I could first confirm I had heard right and then digest this sad piece of information that made me feel like a knife was being thrust into my belly.

What on earth was my own mother telling me? I wondered. *What was I going to tell Auntie who had our baby all this while and was preparing to hand him over to his grandmother?* She also was expecting my mother after speaking to her on the phone; my mum had even prayed for her and thanked her for being a Good Samaritan to us. During the conversation, she had assured Auntie of her imminent arrival in England, so tell me how I was to break the news to Auntie?

It did not make any sense why my mother could not be by my bedside at a time when I needed her most. It is only a natural expectation of first-time mothers to have their mums come over to help when they have their babies; in my case I had expected that she would be on the next plane to Birmingham, knowing I had just undergone surgery on my fractured spine.

After she talked, I did not know what to say and all I could do was cry. I cried a lot and was livid with God and of course with my mum for neglecting me at such a time. Oh yes, I know God speaks and acts in ways we humans can't understand or question but I had to question this one, over and over and over again! *Why did it have to be this time when I needed help from her that He chose to tell her not to visit me?* I wondered. *What could His reasons be? Was there more behind this that I did not know?* I could not get my head around any of it.

The day after surgery, I felt different in my body. It felt like surgery had been done on my chest and not my back because when I tried to move, my entire chest area felt heavy and tight, as though a thick metal plate was affixed to it and was being pulled from all sides. I could barely move my hands and in fact was advised by the nurses not to because of the delicate nature of the surgery. *I wish this was one of my dreams*, I thought, but no, this was real!

I wondered what was going on inside my body and desperately needed to speak to a doctor so I was glad when the registrar accompanied by a team of junior practitioners showed up during their rounds later that day. They seemed pleased to tell me about my grand surgical operation which they had witnessed while I was keen to barrage them with tons of questions.

"Why do I feel this way?" I asked. "When would I begin to walk again? How soon would I be allowed to go home?"

After they managed to provide answers to my urgent questions, I was told that I must lie on my back continuously for at least a week in order to let the surgical work done stay in place. Instructions continued to get rolled out to me. As I was not allowed to move my hands, I could not feed myself and so was fed by hospital staff or Edwin when he visited. I drank fluids from a straw and the cleaning of my body was done daily by the hospital staff. When they needed to clean me, two people would roll me over to my side, making me moan due to the pain inflicted.

Immediately after surgery, I was put on a cocktail of medicines that included vancomycin, ethambutol, Rifater, and pyridoxine hydrochloride, to name a few. I was also administered morphine, codeine, and diclofenac at different times to help alleviate the terrible pains I was battling. Despite the fact that it was never pleasant pushing down up to fifteen tablets at a time, I faithfully took my medications because I was told they worked hand-in-hand with my bones fusing and healing properly. By now, I was prepared to get well at any cost!

A few days later I finally saw my hero, the neurosurgeon who led my operation. He was on his routine ward round and so came to my room to see how I was doing and to explain what he had done. It was only when he began to tell me about the procedure that I was able to paint a better picture.

"The MRI scan you had prior to surgery showed your spine was infected," said the surgeon. "And there was multiple vertebrae collapse on the fourth, fifth, sixth and seventh thoracic (T4-T7) bones of your spine."

As if he sensed that I could not quite comprehend the medical jargon, he drew a quick sketch of the spine on paper, showing the arrangement of these bones.

"There was a full collapse in T4–T6 while T7 had partially collapsed," he explained. "From this, I suspect the cause to be Tuberculosis—"

"No!" I said, cutting short his explanation that a test would be carried out on the sample taken from the pus around my spine in order to verify his hypothesis. "It is impossible for me to have TB!" I spoke with as much conviction as my feeble voice could allow.

It had to be impossible for me to have contracted TB! I thought. I had lived in England for over four years and England as far as is public knowledge, is a place where TB is not prevalent. More so, I had not been to Nigeria or any other TB-endemic country since my wedding in July 2007. From my knowledge of biology—a subject I was proud to have an A grade in—people who were infected with TB ought to depict one main symptom: coughing, sometimes with blood. And since the bout of coughing I had prior to childbirth, I had not really coughed at all. Plus, if I indeed did have TB, where in the world was it known to reside in the spine, of all places?

"It is not possible for me to have TB," I said again.

The poor man must have been taken aback as I uttered those few words amidst my frantic musings.

"Okay, Mrs Ikolo," he said. "Through the process of laminectomy, we took out most of the fractured bones, the infected discs and surrounding tissues of the collapsed vertebrae. While we await the test results, I have prescribed a broad spectrum antibiotic that should cure you of whatever the disease is."

Although I felt he said this simply to make me shut my mouth and not bother him anymore about my knowledge on TB, I was not yet giving up.

"But Doctor, the CT scan and the sputum test done at Good Hope Hospital only last month came back negative so how can I have TB?" I asked.

"Perhaps they were looking for a blood clot or pulmonary TB (TB found in the lungs) and so when they did not see that, they missed this," he said.

He explained that after taking out the infected bits, he screwed two six-millimetre titanium rods into the top and bottom of my spine between T3 and T8 in order to support my bones, leaving them to fuse naturally. Hearing that I had metal rods in my back scared the life out of me and made me ponder how the whole arrangement looked, but I feared even more to ask to see the x-ray images.

Listening to my surgeon talk of the fractured bones in my spine explained the bulge my friend had noticed in the middle of my back when she massaged it in an attempt to alleviate the pain; the bulge was indeed in the area where the scan showed that my spine had collapsed!

Regardless of my insistence that I was not infected with TB, I let the doctors do their job so far as it would make me feel well again. Given they felt I had TB, they thought it necessary to isolate me in order to avoid infecting others. So, right after surgery I was kept in a private room on the East Ground A floor of the QE, with the door always shut. Hospital staff members were advised to always wear aprons and nose masks as a precaution while I was asked not to entertain visitors, including my baby, and if they must visit, they also had to put on protective clothing. Edwin was stubborn and refused to do so. Not long after this they confirmed that it was safe for anyone to be in close contact with me because it had been established from test results and the fact that I was not coughing that the TB was extrapulmonary, meaning it was outside my lungs and so not contagious.

I was over the moon when Auntie brought my baby to visit me in hospital days later. As I was only able to lift his hand slightly, with teary eyes I kissed it and stroked his cute little face over and over again for the few moments he was at my bedside. As if he could understand, I apologised for not being there for him at a time he needed me most. JD looked different and had lots of rashes on his forehead; I must have sounded a bit worried when I asked Auntie what caused it, but she quickly allayed my fears, saying it was only a natural occurrence with babies.

A week after surgery I was told that the long-awaited day for me to be helped to my feet had come. I did not know what to make of this when the physiotherapist explained what I should expect. She said that for the walking rehabilitation, I would be helped to my feet and the feeling would be quite different given it had been a while since I was vertical. The day was daunting as two physiotherapists helped me stand up from my bed. It was an experience I will not forget in a hurry. *Quite different did she say? This is hell!* I muttered quite angrily.

"I'd like to lie down," I said to the physiotherapist because as they had rightly advised, I felt woozy shortly after I stood up.

Not being able to walk unaided frustrated me. I was discouraged and I'd had enough. I knew gaining full use of my legs would take time because the doctor was upfront with me about it, but being in a position where I wanted to be fit but was faced with a painful and difficult road to recovery did not help at all. Moreover, it was terribly painful getting out of bed and attempting to stand, let alone walking with aid.

How can they ask me to exercise my legs when they know how painful it is for me? I wondered. I was no longer prepared to be subjected to such. The whole thing made me angry.

I lost my interest in the entire rehabilitation process and the next time I was asked to do it, I remained stuck to my bed not wanting to do anything I'd been advised to do. One day, whilst consumed by my sadness, a nurse who I believe was originally from the Philippines came to me and told me off.

"Do you want to get well or you want to become one of the furniture here?" she asked me.

I nodded, not knowing where she was going with the question.

"Well, if you want to get well, you have to help yourself and cooperate with the staff here who are doing their very best to help you walk again," the nurse said.

How could she say such hurtful words to me knowing full well my situation? But luckily and thankfully, I saw through the words, understanding her intent. I strongly believe she was used by God to make me literally get off my backside because up until this moment, I had not realised that I had given up.

It was a turning moment for me and felt as if scales were suddenly removed from my eyes. I began to see possibilities instead of limitations. I realised I had truly given up on ever walking again and because of the unbearable pain emanating from my back, I had not wanted to go on with the exercises. But I now had resolve and was determined to get out of hospital and be a mother to my son, just as I had dreamt all those months before he was even conceived. I also began to picture me with him, going to the shopping malls and doing all the other nice things I had imagined doing with him; it gave me the will to fight. Days later, although my legs were still numb, I became less fearful and cooperated with the physios during the exercises; for me and even the staff, this was a great achievement.

I felt I was making some progress generally. My bowels had opened up quite well and so I no longer relied on the catheter and bedpan but instead was usually wheeled to the toilet; for routine tests, I continued to be transported on a stretcher.

To say that I was able to pray during this time would be an utter lie for I was full of pain and too sad to utter a word of prayer. I was grateful, however, for my friends and family who I knew were constantly praying for me. Being unable to pray let alone study my Bible, I knew I needed additional strength to get me through each day in hospital. I got what I call a dose of inspirational maternal calls and messages from my mother who made it a duty to call me every single day I was in hospital. Most times she called me twice a day, once in the morning just after my breakfast and again at night.

"So-oo, how are you today? Have you eaten?" my mum would ask before going on to encourage me that all will be well. Those golden calls she made, which must have cost her a fortune due to the frequency of them, were not wasted and neither were the calls from my sisters, who all reside in Nigeria. They all gave me strength to go through each day.

One thing I did not know then that my sisters told me later was that my mother, who rang me daily to encourage me to eat and not worry, was suffering too. I was told she was not eating but cried every day about her poor, sick daughter whom she could not physically help. Given she is not a young woman, her health was beginning to be affected as a result and her blood pressure spiked up but, thankfully, this came under control. This was the touch of a mother I yearned for, that which no husband, friend, or even sibling could give.

My recollections of the dreams I had prior to and during the early stage of pregnancy also gave me a lot of strength and something to look forward to beyond my current predicament. In one particular dream, I was about seven weeks pregnant and an old friend whom I had not seen nor spoken to in five years rang me up to say God had asked her to tell me that my unborn child would be a healthy child and bring joy and prosperity to us. From the minute I had the dream, up until that moment lying on my hospital bed, I held onto my own perceived meaning of it so dearly and kept replaying the scene in my mind.

Edwin visited me each day and having a family member by my side meant a lot to me. If he visited during my mealtimes, he fed me and also prayed with me before going back home. During his lunch break at work, he usually called to check on me and the one time he did not do so— nor had he come to visit me at the usual time that evening— hell broke loose. I panicked and wondered what could have happened to him, imagining all sorts of dreadful calamities. Unknown to me, he had gone to purchase a new phone for me because mine had suddenly stopped working the day before and as he knew that receiving calls and messages from friends and family kept me going, he did not want me to spend another day without a phone. Only heaven knows how glad I was to see him walk through the hospital door that evening!

As the number of days I remained in hospital grew, so did my concern for my son. Auntie could no longer take care of him so I became desperate to find someone to take over this huge responsibility, especially now we knew my mum was no longer coming over. Being far from Nigeria and having no family member living in England was a major challenge to us. If I did think of running away to care for my son, my partial paralysis prevented me.

Edwin and I resorted to ringing up the few friends we had in town and after some calls were made, a member of my church, Mosun, who was relatively new in town, agreed to look after JD for just that weekend. So on the 3rd of

October 2008, JD was in his third home within the four-and-a-half weeks since he was born. He stayed there for two days and was then taken to our house to be looked after by my dear friend Ada, who travelled down from London with her one-year-old son. I did not expect her to volunteer to come because she was heavily pregnant, but when she did I was grateful. It put my mind at peace, at least for a time and it also gave Edwin the opportunity to be close to our son. Before she went back to London, she came with JD to visit me in hospital, bringing me home-cooked food. I was overjoyed to see my dear son for the first time in over a week. I could not help but notice how much his face had changed. He looked so dark and I hardly recognised him. I was overcome with a flood of emotions and again could not stop crying and apologising to him, even though he was fast asleep most of the time they were there.

I had now been in hospital for two weeks and I did not want to have my baby go live elsewhere. Knowing Ada could only stay in Birmingham for so long due to her family and personal commitments, I again pleaded with my surgeon to let me go home. I made all the promises I could to him, assuring him that I would not lift a finger, but he flatly refused. His fear was that I would easily and naturally want to mother JD and it would have a dire consequence on the recovery of my back. So I had to choose between my back and my baby. Being unsuccessful at convincing him, we could only hope a Good Samaritan would yet again offer to look after our son. Again we made contact with friends and church members and were elated when one of the pastors in church offered to take our son to their home.

Though I was unhappy to let my son live elsewhere than with his parents, particularly because I did not know some of these people too well at the time, I wasn't worried. I knew somehow that he was being looked after by someone above and, honestly speaking, I hadn't much choice so I had to put my faith to work and trust God like I never had, believing He would bring me joy regardless of the current sadness that filled my heart.

Despite the fact that I was not in a delivery ward, I seemed to have constant reminders of my son no matter where I turned. Because I was getting better, I was taken into the main ward with other women. At night there was a particular old lady whose breathing, strangely, reminded me of my new baby's. This used to make me sob quietly for a good few minutes before I drifted off to sleep. Another time, the ladies were having a banter, taking turns telling one another what brought them to the neurosurgical unit of the QE. From what they said, I learnt one had been diagnosed with a brain tumour that had been successfully removed while another, a mum of a considerable number of young children, regretfully said her condition was a lost case of paralysis. Her ordeal reminded me of one more reason to be thankful: had Auntie not taken the initiative to make the 999 call that Sunday morning, a time when both Edwin and I had completely lost faith in the National Health Service and the doctors lack of diagnosis of the cause of my illness, I would have been in the same shoes. As a matter of fact, my surgeon told me he would never have been able to guarantee the recovery of my legs if I had delayed going to hospital. It eventually became my turn to tell my story, and "my baby, my baby" was all I heard myself say. Without sparing a second I burst into fits of tears right after. The ladies were astonished and sorry they had asked me the question.

The biopsy results from the sample taken from around my spine tested positive for TB. Again, this news did not make sense to me.

TB is spread when one inhales tiny droplets from the coughs or sneezes of an infected person and is caused by a bacterium called Mycobacterium tuberculosis. In Nigeria, this illness was known to be prevalent in the remote areas and in the northern part where I did not live. Yes, I had schooled in the south with a number of girls who came from the north but that was over twenty years ago. Plus, my three siblings and I attended the same boarding school at different times, each over a period of six years, so why would it be only me and not also them who contracted the disease?

Going further back in time, in my last year at primary school I suffered my first back pain. My mum, who usually did the school drop off, had taken us to school that morning and after my sisters had jumped out of the car, I struggled to follow them.

"Esosa, will you get out and go to your class?" my mum ordered.

"I can't, Mummy. I can't move!" I said, but she did not believe me and thought I was making up the story in order to get back home to the snacks left over from the workshop which was being held in her office.

"I said get out," said my mum again.

When she saw I remained still regardless of her order, she was forced to drive me to her office. Getting there, she realised I was not teasing after all because I remained stuck to my seat, so she asked one of her staff to carry me to her office. Only after some hours, and not minutes, did I have some relief. This pain came back at various other times and it became known to me and my family that I suffered from occasional back pain.

Spinal Tuberculosis (ST), my affliction, shows up as persisting back pains so recalling this episode of pain, I questioned if I could have had TB in me since I was ten years old and it did not show up until now. Could this have been the first sign of ST and no one realised it? As a teenager, I also used to spit a lot and this habit greatly annoyed my sisters so much that they forced me to go do several sputum tests. I happily took the tests, as I also wanted to know what was causing the irritating habit and have it sorted. Although I can't recall what my sputum was tested for, I know they all came out negative.

I also wondered if TB was contracted during my visit home in 2005. It was my first visit home since coming to England in November 2003. I vaguely recall that in late 2006/early 2007, after getting my first job in Sunderland post-graduation, I began to have recurring pains in my back. Those pains were always unbearable and I used to hate wearing a bra because just around my bra strap line was where I felt the pain most; due to that I was sometimes forced to undo my bra straps in order to have some relief.

So did I have TB then, too? Such was the deluge of unanswerable questions that filled my mind as I continued to ponder my condition and cooperate with the hospital staff in order to get well enough to be discharged.

In my case, TB was not evident and this was why I did not seem to have any of its symptoms; it only became active due to my low immunity—thanks to being pregnant. With latent TB, the onset of symptoms is usually subtle and disease progression is slow. When it becomes active, the symptoms of pulmonary TB include weakness, weight loss, chills, fever and night sweats, loss of appetite, prolonged coughing and breathlessness. The final two symptoms were present in my last stage of pregnancy, but luckily (or perhaps unluckily) I was cleared of pulmonary TB by the two tests done at Good Hope Hospital and the QE. Extrapulmonary TB, on the other hand, is also characterised by the nonspecific symptoms listed above as well as symptoms specific to the organ it lives in; in my situation these were seizures, acute back pain, a deformed spine, difficulty in walking and paraplegia—the loss of feeling and movement in the legs. I remember not eating much, but naturally, I had every reason to think this was due to pregnancy. One other thing I did not realise, which my friends who visited at different times of my illness pointed out, was how much weight I had lost. Looking at my pictures, I do agree with them.

Although my surgeon did not think the TB had been there for years, research tells me that TB can be present in a person for years and even decades before it comes to light. According to my surgeon, he's had patients with ST who came from TB-prevalent areas such as India and, being doctors themselves, they straightaway realised that the TB had developed resistance through being in a TB-prevalent environment. It was only when they moved to a country where TB was uncommon that the disease became active.

My surgeon, who has many years of practical experience in this sort of thing and is, in fact, recognised as one of the best in the region, said that in all his many years of treating patients with ST, he had never come across a pregnant woman with the disease. Indeed finding pregnant women with ST is quite rare worldwide; I believe I am one of the few cases that exists. There is a known study of three pregnant women who were diagnosed with ST in America. While two of them were managed by urgent caesarean sections followed by spinal fusion, one was not as fortunate and had a spontaneous abortion. TB is a serious condition and can lead to death if not treated, so when I say I am grateful to be alive, I mean it!

Although now growing at a somewhat faster rate, Potts disease (another name for ST) is uncommon in developed countries such as the US, and Europe when compared with other endemic areas. To further bring this into perspective, in 2009 a published report gives the account of a pregnant Kenyan woman who presented a year's history of low back pain that started after a fall. An MRI scan revealed she had ST. This report further shows a comparison between the number of cases of ST in America and in Kenya: 4 cases out of a population of 100,000 in a year to 384 cases out of the same population in a year, with it occurring more often in men than women.

Researching and reading about symptoms like night sweats and chills makes me recall a time early on in my pregnancy. In April, on the 17th to be precise, it seemed my usual pregnancy symptoms were being overtaken by more severe ones: I had burning eyes and intermittent chills and fevers; one minute I would be hot and take off my clothes, while the next I would be putting layers back on. I was nauseated and had also been vomiting and coughing a bit with some streaks of blood evident, so with these rather disturbing symptoms, I paid my GP a visit. He diagnosed me to be suffering from dehydration and a possible infection. I can't recall him prescribing any medicines but when I got home, the symptoms became bad enough that I had to call an ambulance. I got admitted into Good Hope Hospital, where I continued to suffer with no help because it was a weekend and the laboratory staff who would carry out the required tests did not work on weekends. On the following Monday, the results of my test finally came and confirmed what my GP had earlier diagnosed; it revealed I had water (bladder) infection and so was put on a course of antibiotic and discharged the next day. Although some of the symptoms of TB can imitate several other illnesses, I cannot help but wonder if this was in any way related to the TB that was already living in me.

I did not give up pestering my surgeon about getting discharged until finally he said he would consider it only if I could tell him I had someone to help me when I went home. I assured him that I would, which was true because after we'd accepted that my mum was not coming, she suggested my younger sister visit instead, especially as she was on holiday from the university at the time. Thus, I asked my surgeon to write us a letter stating that I urgently needed help from my family due to my illness; with his letter, coupled with other necessary documents we had collated and sent to my sister, things were now in motion to get her a visa. With all this we were hopeful she would get her visa and would be with us in no time, so I became excited.

The staff at QE was good to me and such acts of kindness made me feel like God was smiling down at me, letting me know He was with me. For instance, there was a lovely lady who used to come round the ward twice a day to serve tea and coffee. She was always, and I mean always, smiling while doing this job. I remember I always looked forward to her tea rounds when I would ask for my favourite cup of hot chocolate drink served with biscuits. She was such a breath of fresh air and one day before I got discharged I asked her for her name. We got talking a bit more and I learned that not only is she a Christian, but that we attend the same church and had never met before! We became friends from that day onwards and she ended up baking me a cake for Jedidiah's dedication many months later.

Another act of kindness happened during that time when I hadn't heard from Edwin all day and panicked. The ward matron came round to check on me and saw me looking forlorn. After I told her my reason for being upset, she immediately offered me her personal mobile phone to call Edwin. It was moments of kindness like these that made what I was going through more bearable.

Chapter 5

Although it felt much longer, I was eventually signed off after almost three weeks in the QE. Before letting me leave, I was told a list of things I could and couldn't do and these, I must say, terrified me, actually causing me to think twice about leaving hospital. I was not allowed to hold or lift up my baby and other than when I needed to eat or go to the bathroom, I should only sit up for a maximum of ten minutes in every given period, after which I must lie back down. This truly freaked me out, but the thought of being with my baby again was something I really looked forward to.

The paramedics took me home in an ambulance on a somewhat bumpy and airy ride because their Satnav misdirected them, landing me in front of the wrong block of flats. Luckily, I was able to identify where we were, so off they carried me on a stretcher round a few blocks until we safely made it to my block.

I arrived home during the day and as Edwin was at work, he had arranged with a lady from church, Antoinette, to receive me. Once settled into my home, I needed to take my usual concoction of medicines and then noticed I had not been given my dose of the painkiller co-codamol. Realising I would not be able to cope, I immediately rang up the hospital and spoke with the nurse on duty. She was very apologetic and sent it through a taxi driver within the hour.

Given we had previously contacted the family who had our son, by the evening of that same day, they brought JD home where he belonged. Words are not sufficient to describe the magical moment this was. I was grateful, to say the least.

Antoinette reminded me of my sisters in a number of ways for she took such great care of me. While she was in the house that weekend and at other times she visited, she did anything and everything including cleaning the house, sorting out the laundry and dressing me. Sometimes, after all these tasks, she still had the strength to take JD out in his pushchair for a walk by the lakeside. Having an extra person in the house to help with things was an additional blessing and whenever it was time for Antoinette to return to her house at the end of each visit, I was unhappy. When I became strong enough to sit up for more than ten minutes, she would wash and style my hair and tell me lovely stories about growing up with her sisters in Grenada. Those stories reminded me a lot of my own life with my sisters.

A familiar challenge set in on the first Sunday evening when Antoinette said she had to resume work in the new week. I knew what this meant and my concern was heightened, given Edwin would also go to work come Monday morning. It reminded me of those initial days when I was alone with JD after leaving Good Hope Hospital. I knew this time that if I damned the consequences and disobeyed the doctor's strict post-surgery instructions, I would end up back in hospital. I did not want that, but our hands were tied.

Edwin's working pattern during that time was on a rota, with an 8 a.m. start to 4 p.m. for the first three weeks of the month and then 1–9 p.m. for the fourth week. With no success in getting anyone to help, we made do with what we had. It was the second week in October, which meant Edwin finished work by 4 p.m. and would be home at the latest by 5 p.m. Before leaving that morning, he prepared two portions of formula milk in bottles which he kept in a food warmer right next to my bedside. These portions were expected to last until he got back. Because he had fed JD right before leaving the house that morning, JD's next feed was not until two to three hours later and, come this time, I managed to give him the first bottle lying down. Shortly after, he slept off. I was well informed of the practice of winding a baby after each feed but as I could only lie down and not lift things, this good practice of releasing trapped air went out the window.

When it was time for his next feed in the afternoon, my mothering instincts would not allow me to give him the nearly cold and most likely stale second bottle of milk so I took the bull by the horns and made my way to the kitchen using my crutches. To save time, I decided to use the microwave to heat up some water for the milk. With my arm close to my chest and a gentle thrust of my body, I pressed the microwave button. The pain I felt is better imagined. Surgery was performed on the thoracic region, which is from about shoulder level to halfway down the back; so, by this subtle action, I was literally stretching the still-sore muscles.

After Edwin got home from work that evening, he searched through his phone directory, calling different people and asking if they might be available for the days ahead. I had been attending Mount Zion Community Church for just over a year while Edwin joined seven months after me, so although I could not really say that many people knew us, we were known by a handful. A few months after joining the church, a friend, Bose, whom I met on the first day I relocated to Birmingham, invited me to one of the church's cell group meetings; this was a forum for church members to meet and fellowship in each other's houses in small groups. Through these meetings I made a few new friends so they were the people I advised Edwin to contact first. Unfortunately, not one of them was available to help me during the day due to work commitments but, in the nick of time, a lady to whom I'd never spoken in church said she could help on the odd day when she was free! With Egnetia's offer, my day with JD was better and things improved even more a few days later when another lady, Jasmine, offered to also come one day a week, making it two days covered!

Edwin was doing his best to take care of both of us when he got home from work. His routine was basically the same every day over the period I was incapacitated. Before leaving for work he would prepare our meals for the day and feed JD. He also would place everything I would need at a reachable distance and, when back from work, resume his duties. He attended to JD's needs first—changing his nappy, feeding and bathing him. Next, he'd give me a bath and thereafter feed me before he had any time for himself.

It would have been great if Edwin could've worked from home or adjusted his working hours to night time but I knew this was, to some extent, a selfish wish due to the nature of his work, so I had to stick to reality and be grateful for what I had.

Over the period of time of my recovery, Edwin and I noticed that JD was bringing up his food after each feed and although we cannot say if this was linked to how we fed him in a lying position during those times I was alone with him, we knew this was not right; he was hardly retaining any food. We spoke to our doctor who, after advising us to change his formula milk which did not seem to help, also asked that we hold him up for a minimum of thirty minutes after each feed to allow the food to go and stay down. This seemed to help.

We decided not to keep JD in his cot bed for two reasons: one was because I would not be able to get him out if I needed to attend to him; and the second, to afford the two of us time to bond. Despite how I felt, I always tried to smile at JD reassuringly whenever he looked at me in between sleeps, wearing one of his innocent smiles. I also would try to reach out to him and stroke his face before he drifted off to his next round of sleep

Before leaving hospital and as part of her job, the physiotherapist was concerned about my adaptation to certain things in my house. One thing she did to ensure I adapted quite well was ask my husband to furnish her with the dimensions of my bed. With that information, she was able to tell that the dimensions were right, so the hospital did not need to provide me with a new bed. They did, however, give me a commode to place over my toilet seat to help my balance when using the toilet. In addition, I was given a pair of crutches, a brown leather armchair to use when I needed to eat and a pick-up tool, similar to that used by bin men to pick up litter on the street, to help me get things on the floor or out of my reach without bending. I am grateful that the physiotherapists at QE knew their job, because when I got home I found all of these things very useful.

Without trying to exaggerate the discomfort I was having, I was not in a good place having to cope with the pains from both the illness and as a result of surgery. At one time I felt that the screws were poking and pinching my skin and this made me uncomfortable. I believed I needed a change of mattress so we purchased an orthopaedic one but this did not improve things. I feared the screws had become loose and I dreaded what the outcome would be if this was true. I could not help feeling something would happen to my back that would make me end up on the surgeon's table again, so I was in the habit of asking Edwin to inspect it so that if my fear was right, I would know immediately.

Furthermore, due to the tension from the rods and screws, I constantly felt as if the metalwork was fixed right across my back.

"Eddie, could you please check to see if you can feel the metalwork or anything out of place across my back?" I often said.

"Esosa, relax. A signboard was not inserted into your back," he replied, half teasing, those times he bothered to actually look and answer me.

Other times I was curious to know what my back looked like and I'd ask Edwin to have a look to see if he could spot any changes. I recall one time after having a look he said the areas flanking my spine looked somewhat darker than normal. We both wondered about this for a while and finally came up with an answer that sounded right, though we never sought any medical opinion: we thought that it must be due to bruising of the still-sore surgical area.

A few days before leaving hospital, I was contacted by a social worker from the Adults and Communities directorate of the Queen Elizabeth Hospital who assessed me and questioned me about my residency status.

"Where are you originally from?" the man asked. "How long have you lived in England?"

"Nigeria and nearly four years," I replied.

From additional questions he asked me, he learned my visa was subject to immigration control and as a result, I had no recourse to public funds; this meant I would not be able to claim any form of benefits or get support from the government. However, he told me his department would be able to fund the provision of support services for me but not for my baby. In his letter to the manager of the Children and Families department, he explained my situation, saying 'the needs of herself and the child deem them to be Destitute-plus—that is, over and above mere destitution'.

In this letter, which I got a copy of, he advised them of Section 54 and Schedule 3 of the Immigration and Asylum Act 2002, which prevents local authorities from providing support under certain conditions, saying it should not apply to me. His recommendation to them was that they should provide support services for my baby, given his department could only cater to my needs. With this, I looked forward to receiving my own support from them, as I was sure that whoever came to help me would be compassionate and also help my baby.

My pastor, Calvin, and his wife visited me and they both were unhappy with the state I was in. He said he did not see why the council could not help so he got in touch with an older member of the church, who I believe had experience with such things. This lovely lady tried her best to find a solution to my situation, but there was no success.

After that time, around late October, I was paid a visit by another social worker from the Young People and Families directorate. During her assessment, the young lady asked me several questions about how I had been coping with my health problems and the baby, and I told her of the challenges. I also told her of the initial attempt by Queen Elizabeth Hospital to secure some support from the council, which was all to no avail. After observing me with my baby for around thirty minutes, she made some notes and left, saying she would discuss my situation with her manager and let me know the outcome. It was no surprise when she contacted me about a week later to say that due to the same clause on my visa, no help would be forthcoming.

It was a blessing to have Egnetia and Jasmine help when they could but, understandably, they could not be there every time I needed them. There were days I struggled with caring for my baby, hoping someone would knock on my door offering a helping hand. Though it was not on a regular basis, I benefited from and was very grateful for the help rendered by friends who came at different times, with some sparing a few hours a day and others a whole day during weekends. I was shown much love from the few friends we had and also from people who, upon hearing my story, were moved to help me. For instance, a friend of mine told me about a lady who lived near me. I had never met her but she was willing to help. She had two young children and was expecting her third but did not mind coming to my house every other week to help clean up and prepare large quantities of delicious meals. I was more than grateful for the latter, given my husband's favourite place is not the kitchen. I also had help from my cell group members who visited occasionally, carrying out different tasks including massaging my back and cleaning of the house. Even after they were finished they often asked for more work!

With it now established that no help was forthcoming from any government office, I anxiously awaited some good news from my younger sister Itohan, who had previously applied for a visitor's visa. And as if the disappointments rolling in during this period were not enough, she called to say her application had been declined. That meant we were again back to square one and Edwin and I recommenced the phone rounds in search of someone to help us on a permanent basis, if possible. In the midst of my disappointments, my mum advised me to make an appeal to the immigration and asylum tribunal, which I did, and after a period of ten months my sister was granted a six month visitor's visa. Although this was victory in a sense, by the time she visited, I had recovered quite well and had even returned to work.

And although it was good to see her, the main aim of her visit had been defeated.

One other thing I was told by the social worker who visited me at home was that they had contacted my baby's health visitor, whose primary role is to work with the community and make home visits to new parents, thus providing them with support they may need. From the discussion they had with her, they discovered alternative support I might be eligible to receive from two charity organisations, Homestart and Surestart. Both charities offer family support to help parents build better lives for their children. They also help families with young children deal with life's challenges. Based on the limited areas covered by Surestart, I was referred to Homestart charity by the health visitor. Days later, I got a call from the manager of Homestart who, after chatting with me and gaining more information about my needs, promised that come the following week, two of their volunteers would come help me two days a week.

I certainly can't recall ever knowing of such organisations. Perhaps I had heard of them during my antenatal classes but dismissed the information because I did not need it. One thing I know is that if I had known of their services earlier, I would have by all means referred myself and by hook or by crook, my baby and I would have become their patients from the word go!

The volunteers came every week on the said two days and they were brilliant. They arrived at 9.30 a.m. and spent three hours each day helping with all sorts of tasks, including bathing my baby, feeding him, and washing and sterilising his bottles while I rested. The time they spent was most appreciated and not once was I disappointed due to a volunteer not showing up. If a volunteer could not make it for any reason, one of their paid office staff or the manager herself would turn up instead. One of the ladies used to sing a lovely lullaby to JD. This was my first time hearing the song "Rock-a-bye Baby" which I liked but did not know the words to. When she realised how hard I was trying to learn the song, she got me the CD. This song eventually became JD's daily dose of lullaby when I became well enough to sing. I still sing it to him and his little brother to this day, with the difference being that they now sing it with me.

Chapter 6

Recovery was gradual even though I remained quite stuck to my bed, and it was late October or early November when I commenced additional home physiotherapy. The physiotherapist came to my house and taught me several exercises to do while lying in bed that would help strengthen my legs, and despite the fact that I was not yet going out, I also learned the skill of using my crutches up and down the stairs. When I started to do these exercises, my legs felt like bags of lead, as they had right from the QE. My new physio was quick to explain that it was due to inactivity and as soon as my mobility improved I would feel better. I really hoped she was right.

One of the exercises I was taught was to lift my leg to a comfortable height and hold it up for some seconds before letting it down. At the start, given I was unable to move my legs let alone lift them up, she used to do this for me. After a while, I was able to do it myself, which was huge progress for me.

Physiotherapy was a new thing to me, considering neither I nor anyone I knew had ever had a need for it.

Consequently, I did not fully comprehend how my legs, which were without sensation, could regain their use. Now knowing about how it helps to strengthen the muscles, I am glad I followed through with the routine exercises.

In a possibly unrelated scenario, I began to notice something odd about my rib cage. At first I did not make anything of it but when that area began to feel heavy and quite sore, I grew concerned.

"Please take a look at this and tell me what you think," I said to Edwin one evening, pointing to the area below my breast.

"This sure doesn't look right," he said.

Of course it did not look right! The left side of my rib cage looked distended. With a confirmation from Edwin, we rang up our GP's surgery the next day and that evening, a GP was sent to me on a home visit.

"Well," said the doctor after a long pause, "I can't tell the root cause."

As he could not figure out what had given rise to it, he simply advised I take the precaution of not lying on my left side. He also said it should get better, and the same thing was said by my physiotherapist when she visited. In her opinion there would be an improvement when I became mobile. One could see how protruding this part of my chest was, even through my clothes. Not knowing what caused it made me uncomfortable and with the pain that had begun to emanate from it and that of my back, I became increasingly concerned. Two days later we called the ambulance instead of leaving it to fate like before.

The ambulance arrived and took Edwin and me to the A & E unit of Good Hope Hospital while Antoinette who was visiting, helped to look after JD. It was six weeks after surgery and my back remained quite sore, so while at the hospital I still needed to carry out my doctor's orders by not sitting up for long. I asked the staff on duty for a bed to lie on while I waited to be attended to, and after what seemed like a good hour or more, one was provided. The doctor assessed me and ordered an x-ray, which came back as normal, showing the rods and screws in the right places. Thank God, for this allayed my previous fears of the screws being loose but I was still left with trying to figure out what was making my rib cage so swollen. I tried not to let it disturb me but I could not help wondering if it was caused by the surgery or perhaps the TB had also affected my ribs, even though no test had proven this to be so. Many thoughts raced through my mind and I made sure to talk to my chest consultant about it during my first chest clinic appointment at Good Hope Hospital later on in December. After examining me, he could not tell me what had caused the swelling but said there was no cause for concern. He called the condition Tietze's syndrome, which he said was benign and would go away after a while.

Although not confirmed, I chose to go with the simple explanation given by my neurosurgeon who said the condition may have been caused as a result of walking bent over due to my collapsed spine, thus putting strain on my rib cage. When I walked, I used to clutch my chest and look down in an attempt to suppress the pain and this posture continued all the way to after surgery. In my opinion, I believe I carried on with this posture also because of fear of if I tried walking or standing straight, the metalwork in my back could snap!

I carried on taking my medicines as advised by my surgeon who said I should take them for nine months. The chest consultant at Good Hope Hospital advised me to take them for six months. With these two different recommendations and recalling a scary story told by my surgeon about a patient they thought was cured of TB after completing a course of the medicines but who had a surprising relapse, I decided to take them for a year. I simply could not afford to take any chances. While taking the concoction of medicines over this entire period, I ensured I consulted my chest consultant so he was aware of what I was taking at every given time. I also had regular home visits by the phlebotomist who checked my blood for a number of things including abnormalities in my organs.

One day, I had a home visit from a nurse at the Birmingham and Solihull Chest Clinic. She said she had come to talk to me about TB and the medicines I was taking. My initial reaction was one of unease given no one had informed me of her visit. I did not feel I should discuss my illness with her but after some minutes of chatting with her, she allayed my concern. This was my first time hearing about the clinic. I found the regular visits from her quite useful as she explained more about the illness, reiterating the need for me to not miss taking my medicines and to complete my dose; otherwise, I stood the risk of the TB coming back. During one of her visits, she observed that the dose of one of my medicines was far less than it should be so she contacted my chest consultant who agreed with her and increased the dose.

The chest clinic, I learned, offers a variety of services relating to allergies, respiratory organs, the heart and the thoracic area. They also carry out surgical procedures on patients. From a later visit I made to the clinic in May 2015, I was told they see a mix of both white and black TB patients, with a greater number of black patients. In their screening clinic, patients are seen on a self-referral basis and as referred by their doctors. The tests to confirm the presence of TB in these patients include a combination of sputum test, blood test, and what is called a tuberculin skin test. The tuberculin skin test is done by injecting a small amount of fluid called tuberculin into the skin and after two to three days, the person returns to the clinic to have trained staff look for a reaction on the arm. This informs them if TB is indeed present.

While I find this practice good, I believe it still poses the challenge of only being able to carry out such tests on patients with suspected pulmonary TB, as it is only with such active TB that the symptoms are more evident.

Still early November and despite the dullness presented by the wintry cold that had begun to kick in, there was a lot of cheery news and discussions happening. Everyone, be they interested in world politics or not, was talking about one subject: the moment in history when Barack Obama became the first African-American to win the presidential seat in America. Though I was still a bit confined to my bed, I could occasionally join friends in the living room for short periods, and even though I hardly joined in the conversations, I was glad these discussions had taken over the silence that usually engulfed my home. The unspoken looks and sighs of pity I got from friends who came over were no more, as people revelled in the political distraction. So, in essence, I was grateful to President Obama for helping take everyone's focus off me. I was proud once again to be an African.

I used to say that if anyone tried pouring a kettle of boiling water on me, I would not feel a thing and this was true. Two months post-surgery, I was still numb from below my breast downwards but, as my surgeon had said that recovery could take a minimum of three months, I continued to look forward to regaining sensation. During the brief periods when I got up to use the bathroom or sat down to eat, I would quickly steal a glance through my bedroom window, admiring people as they walked to catch the bus. This became my new routine, watching pedestrians as they made their way past my flat. My wish was a simple one: to walk again and take my son out on the bus, for I had not known the blessing of being able to walk as such an important gift until I lost it!

JD was a very peaceful baby for which I was grateful; he hardly cried unless he was hungry and thereafter he went all quiet and slept. As a matter of fact, it seemed like all he did was sleep and sometimes I feared and so would nudge him gently just to confirm he was breathing. All the people who helped look after him praised him and said the same and it was at such instances that the meaning of his name—'beloved of the Lord'—came alive to me. I was glad

Edwin insisted on giving him his own choice of name over mine. I realised God had Jedidiah covered and as far as I was concerned, this was why even though Edwin and I were unable to be there for him as his parents, God provided able parents to look after His beloved child.

When I was pregnant I did not know much about babies, but I knew I did not want a crying baby and so this was one particular thing I had prayed for. I had not realised that the nurses used to silently watch me when I attended appointments at the chest clinic in Good Hope Hospital. One day, as I began to feed JD, two of them came to me and said I was a lucky mum for having such a well-behaved baby; one would hardly know he was in his pushchair until I brought out his bottle. Whenever I heard these comments I'd smile, thanking God for answering my prayer, for He knew I had enough on my plate.

As advised numerous times, I took my medicines without fail and, notwithstanding the slow recovery, believed that my healing commenced days after surgery. On various occasions I would feel some kind of movement down my spine to my legs as I lay in bed. It felt like fluid seeping down the middle of my backbone. At first it gave me a weird feeling, but when it happened more than once I became more conscious and then got used to it. This gave me an unexplainable assurance that I was being healed even though this was not really evident. Another time, while still in hospital, I dreamt that I went to welcome my mum at the train station and as I made to stand up and walk towards her with the aid of the crutches, I saw to my surprise that I was able to do so without them.

"Mummy! See? I can walk!" I heard myself shout to her.

I woke up believing this would soon be my story.

The swelling on my left rib cage region was still as prominent and although the pins-and-needles feeling I'd been having on my legs was decreasing, it was easing into the third month of my recovery, so I eagerly awaited the miraculous moment when I would walk again.

I again began to feel the metalwork in my back and this time I was certain that the screws were loose. This unwelcome feeling made me fearful of the consequences, as I could not imagine going under the surgeon's knife again. As if this was not enough to scare me, I started having a sharp pain down my sides and back, different to the pain I had been feeling since surgery. With my constant cry about it, Edwin rang my surgeon's secretary who asked that I come in to the ward that day. I got readmitted to QE on the 10th of December and a series of tests was done, including an MRI scan, but nothing seemed to be wrong. The image showed some difference in the bones, which meant they were healing. I know my surgeon had said that due to the nature and scale of the surgery I should not expect things to go back to the way they were in my back, but as much as I understood his explanation, I had come to a point of not taking any feeling or new symptom at face value but would rather it was checked out thoroughly. After being monitored for two days, I was discharged and advised to carry on taking my medication.

In the morning of the day I got discharged I went to the bathroom as usual, aided by my crutches. After I finished having a bath, I put on my robe and made my way to the door. It was after taking a few steps that it dawned on me:

I did this without using my crutches. I walked there with my very own legs! And as soon as I realised this, it made me jolt with fear; I immediately grabbed my sticks so that I did not fall.

"Hallelujah!" I shouted and could not wait to get back to my ward to ring up Edwin and my family to tell them the good news. It was quite a surreal moment for me to regain the use of my legs in the very same place where I had the corrective surgery. An early Christmas gift this was!

Following this miracle, I continued to gain more use of my legs although they were quite wobbly. Apart from a few visits to the chest consultant at Good Hope Hospital, my baby and I hardly went out and when we did, as I had not regained full balance on my feet, I usually would lean on Edwin if he was with me or use my baby's pushchair for support. Because we did not go out often, it is little wonder that when I became well enough to go out and we took JD to church for the first time on New Year's Eve, he screamed uncontrollably. Shortly after we walked into the main church hall where the music was playing loudly, he started to cry. A friend took him out, and as soon as they were out he would be quiet, but the moment she brought him in, crying resumed. We immediately figured out that this was because he had not seen that many people together since his birth, neither had he heard such loud music. So when I became stronger, I made it my priority to take him out to busy and loud places such as the Bull Ring Shopping Centre, even when I had no need to go out. This self-taught therapy seemed to work as in no time JD had acclimatised.

As I grew stronger, the help from Homestart gradually wound down. We knew it would still be useful to have help in the house, but as we had run out of the kind of help that we could get, coupled with the fact that we just could not afford to pay for a nanny, we did not make this a priority. Edwin usually took JD for his routine health check and also to get my regular supply of TB medicines from the GP. During one of those visits, he met a doctor who is also Nigerian. They got chatting and after he issued a prescription for my routine medicines, he explained to Edwin a bit more about such surgical operations and told him that if we ever needed to ask any questions about it, we should feel free to call him on the number that he gave Edwin. When Edwin told me about this encounter with the rather friendly doctor, I asked him to call him as surprisingly, but truly, I had still not fully accepted the diagnosis of my illness as TB and so wanted to inquire more. True to his word, this doctor paid us a visit and we talked at length about the illness and the fixation done in my back. Within an hour, it felt like we had known each other for many years as I discovered he was schoolmate with a couple of my friends back in Nigeria; plus, I later learnt that my mother knew his late father who was also a medical doctor in Nigeria. A few days after his visit, I was rung up by him and he said that he and his wife were willing to pay for a month of childcare for JD while I concentrated on getting better: another well-timed miracle!

My first scheduled follow-up appointment at Queen Elizabeth Hospital outpatient clinic was in February 2009, four months after my surgery, and I was very eager to know if my back was doing well. After the results of the routine

MRI scan and x-ray, I was asked to go see my surgeon, who was quite pleased to see how well I looked. As if I had not heard it enough, I asked him to replay what he did in my back on the 22nd of September. He kindly explained it all again and showed me both the MRI images taken prior to surgery and the one just taken, and I could quite clearly see the difference. In the previous one, I could see that my vertebrae seemed to be encroaching into the spinal area, which looked squashed, and the area where the affected discs were looked quite spacious. There also seemed to be some irregularly shaped fluid-like matter over the middle area of my spine, with part of it moving into the natural line of the spinal cord.

I knew that I had lost some height due to the removal of the collapsed vertebrae and discs and with my now somewhat bent posture, I was keen to know how much of this had affected the curvature of my spine. On his computer, my surgeon measured the angle of curvature on the x-ray image and, comparing this with that from before surgery, he said there was not much difference. I vaguely recall that he said the curve of my spine measured between 46–48 degrees, which on comparison to the normal curve of the human spine, around 45 degrees, is not so bad.

Chapter 7

According to the World Health Organisation (WHO), 'about one-third of the world's population has latent TB, which means people have been infected by TB bacteria but are not (yet) ill with the disease and cannot transmit the disease'.

Occurring mainly in the lungs, research has now shown that TB can affect other areas of the body such as the lymph nodes, urinary tract, sexual organs, the intestines, kidneys, bones, hips, brain, spine and even the skin. ST causes the glands to swell, with back pain being the earliest and most common symptom, ranging from dull to acute pain. Because TB symptoms range in severity and can affect several body parts, diagnosis on the basis of external symptoms alone is not always possible. This is why the Magnetic Resonance Imaging scan, or MRI scan as it is widely called, is the most valuable diagnostic tool for extrapulmonary TB such as ST as on suspicion of it, the scan shows more of the extent of damage within.

I read an online article which does justice to explaining the relatively low level of awareness people still do have about ST. It was written in October 2014 by a spine doctor in India. He wrote that he had a female patient come to him describing symptoms she'd been having over the past few weeks. These were acute back pain, fever, night sweats and anorexia. She also recounted that she had been facing significant weight loss, pain, and stiffness in her limbs and that her condition was getting worse, to the point that she started having difficulty with sitting and walking. After listening to her outline her symptoms, he immediately told her that she was suffering from TB, and she freaked out.

"Are you kidding me doc? The lady said. Tuberculosis is related to lungs and you are a spine doctor."

"Spinal tuberculosis has become very common these day but people are not aware about it and neglect the symptoms associated with it," the doctor told her.

And with an MRI scan, ST was indeed confirmed in the patient.

Similarly, ST could be misinterpreted as other illnesses due to its very similar symptoms. Like it was for me a person may be ill with ST and just doesn't realise it. In another online medical journal, a patient who had been suffering from acute waist pain and partial paralysis of one side of his upper and lower limbs visited his GP, and he was immediately diagnosed to have stroke. Following this initial diagnosis and treatments at a tertiary institution he was referred to, he did not get better. With increasingly severe pains in his waist accompanied by incontinence and difficulty in standing, he was referred to another hospital. This time he was fortunate to receive proper medical care and with the use of MRI scan, he was diagnosed with spinal tuberculosis.

Unlike then, I now know that early diagnosis of ST may be difficult when associated with pregnancy because the disease can mimic some of the physiological changes that occur during pregnancy, such as extreme tiredness, increased respiratory rate, fatigue, cough, weight loss, fever, etc. For me, TB was latent for however long until my pregnancy developed, so I quite understand why anyone, myself included, could have misinterpreted or overlooked the symptoms. What I find hard to understand is why no one cared to respond correctly to the result from the scan done on the 19th of August that showed my lymph nodes were enlarged. Lymph nodes are oval in shape and are distributed widely throughout the body, including the throat, armpit and stomach. They are an important part of the immune system and become visible and conspicuous when inflamed by various infections and diseases.

As I later learnt from my medical records, this same scan report as documented by the radiographer contained the following information:

'The pulmonary arterial circulation enhances normally with no evidence to suggest a pulmonary embolism. There is a 17 x 24 mm diameter lymph node at the right hilum which is pathologically enlarged and a pre-tracheal 15 mm diameter lymph node. Some minor atelectasis is present in both lung bases and there is possibly a minimal pleural reaction at the right base. There is a significant collapse of a mid dorsal vertebral body, probably D7, and a lytic process in the posterior aspect of the lower vertebral body, probably D8. On the axial images, there is a soft tissue reaction surrounding these vertebral bodies which measures up to

16 mm in diameter, and this extends laterally around and behind the aorta.'

The conclusive notes of the radiographer said there was suspicion of TB and that I should be referred to a chest physician. After reading this, I did not quite understand most of the medical jargon used, so I immediately resorted to using Google, and by inputting the key words I got this explanation. In my own layman's interpretation, the scan showed I had enlarged lymph nodes at the base of my right lung. Atelectasis refers to a condition in which one or more areas of the lungs collapse or don't inflate properly. Pleural reaction is either an inflammation of the pleura which is the covering for the lungs, or an increased accumulation of pleural fluid. Joining the dots, I realised that this report actually says I had some sort of collapse in my lungs, which makes me a little confused about what sort of TB I had. Mid dorsal vertebral D7 and D8 are the same as the thoracic T7 and T8 of the spine, with D7 being one of the four vertebrae shown by the MRI scan to be actually infected and collapsed.

Realising what this report was indeed saying shocked me beyond my wits. If this was true, why then was I discharged from Good Hope Hospital and classed as being medically fit to go home? And if this clearly important information came out of the initial CT scan I had done at the same hospital in August, why then was I told only the bit about enlarged lymph nodes, as though there was no other finding? Was it that the rest was seen as trivial?

I had a friend who had one of her lungs collapse and I know how badly she suffered, so pardon me for being alarmed at reading this piece of shocking information about my own body. Did I indeed have some sort of collapse in my lungs and yet my consultant knew of it and did nothing to expedite my treatment? Was it a question of poor communication or the lack of it? What is the reporting channel that was inadequate? Who should be informed and who should be advising whom?

My shock did not end here as I later came across notes by two other consultants. The first was written on the 27th of August by the respiratory consultant who said that the same scan showed my chest was clear and that I had hila lv and a lytic process in my dorsal spine plus underlying spine osteomyelitis. The other consultant, who is a haematology specialist, wrote that 'it would be difficult and unusual to associate her dorsal vertebra damage to HBAS'. He then interpreted the same results as being signs caused by one of the following: TB, lymphoma (cancer of the lymph nodes), myeloma (cancer of the bone marrow), sarcoidosis (a disease caused by enlarged lymph nodes) or infective discitis (infection of the intervertebral disc space). He recommended that there was no need for me to undergo an MRI scan but instead I should be referred for a tissue biopsy to be carried out on my lymph nodes a week after delivery.

Had these notes mentioned the presence of flu-like symptoms or allergies, I would not have been alarmed, but these were serious ailments that if any of my friends or a family member was diagnosed with today, would send everyone running amok! Surely there were more than enough pointers showing that what could have made me sick was certainly not caused by pregnancy. For consultants who were privy to the full report of my CT scan to overlook it and not pay any attention to my ailing situation is highly unprofessional. That my gynaecologist was advised of such severe potential causes of my illness plus the need for me to undergo a biopsy a week after childbirth and yet, despite our pleas to remain in hospital, still sent us home five days after childbirth is totally appalling!

Perhaps I would not have had to undergo surgery had more attention been given to the report. I might have just had to wear braces and be on bed rest for a given period while taking the TB medication. Better still, I may not have had to carry these foreign bodies called rods. Yes, the long-awaited letter referring me for endoscopy came about the second or third week in October, after I had undergone surgery, but it was of no use because if I had waited at home until then, what would have become of me? I can't help but wonder why a duty of care to provide me with the full information about my scan and blood results was not carried out.

Knowledge is indeed power! From what I have read and also experienced, 'almost every pregnant woman experiences back pain during pregnancy and 'this is so because a certain hormone called relaxin makes the strong supporting ligaments in a woman's back become softer during pregnancy. Similarly, 'about all pregnant women who experience back problems during pregnancy are able to labour normally during childbirth, and only in exceptional cases do some who have severe back problem need to have a planned C-section'.

I believe it was due to my constant complaints of pains that my gynaecologist suggested I should have a C-section—a decision which made me unhappy as I had desired to give birth naturally. When for a reason unknown to me this decision was changed to having an induced labour, I believed my prayers had been answered.

Upon reading my medical notes years later which say that there was significant collapse possibly in D7 and a probably lytic process (damage) in D8, I became curious. I wondered if as the scan result showed damage to only these two bones, it could be that by this time, the other bones (T4-T6) had not collapsed, as was later revealed by the MRI scan done at Queen Elizabeth hospital. If yes, does this mean that the continuous subjection of my spine to the pregnancy induced back pain, and more so labour, expedited its collapse? I still can't fathom why there was a lapse of ten whole days from when the CT scan result was provided to when I was induced to give birth, when my consultants were fully informed of a number of potential causes of my ill health. *Was it that the information from the scan report was withheld from my gynaecologist?* I wondered. *What exactly could have happened? If indeed I suffered from any of the suspected illnesses as suggested by the haematology consultant, why would he go on to advise against an MRI scan—the one thing that could have accurately confirmed his suspicion?* It made no sense to me.

The same haematology consultant who recommended that I should be referred for a tissue biopsy, also advised that the tissue sample needed should be taken off my body if I end up having a C-section done. *Does this explain why my gynaecologist initially suggested I have a C-section and so had nothing to do with the pains I had? If so, why did he change his mind? Was it because he did not believe the suspicions of the consultant?*

Assuming the consultant's suspicion of any of those illnesses was correct, like I now know, tissue biopsy can actually reveal abnormalities including infection caused by TB. What I do not know is if it would have done so considering I had extrapulmonary TB. Be that as it may, this was a valuable recommendation and why it was not adhered to beats me again! Surely it was not because one ignorant pregnant woman insisted on having a natural delivery that made my gynaecologist change his mind, for even though I was keen on living out my desire, I couldn't have stood in his way had he insisted on a C-section. Yes, I was being tortured by the pains but surely it would have been a no-brainer to agree to it if it meant that I would have been spared additional torture!

Chapter 8

Even though he did not show any symptoms, I naturally became concerned that my baby could have contracted TB and so, during one of my visits to my GP, I asked about it being a possibility. He said no because my son had been given the BCG injection at birth. While I appreciated his response, I was not satisfied with it because I also was given the same vaccine as a baby but contracted TB. With a burning quest to understand more, I brought up the subject during my visit to the chest clinic in May. After asking the same question, the nursing manager explained that although commonly used as a preventive form of TB, the BCG vaccination is no longer one hundred percent reliable and, as research now shows, it is effective against severe forms of the disease, such as TB meningitis in children, but not as effective against all forms of TB. Regardless of this limitation, medical advice is still to have a BCG injection soon after birth as it will continue to be an important tool in the global fight against TB until new vaccines are available.

As a known fact, not everyone infected with TB bacteria becomes sick. With the two TB-related conditions, TB infection being one and the active TB disease itself being the other, many people who have latent TB infection never develop TB disease while some people may develop the disease within weeks of becoming infected, before their immune system can fight the TB bacteria. Others may get sick much later when their immune system becomes weak, as was in my case. WHO states that 'tuberculosis is second only to HIV/AIDS as the greatest killer worldwide due to a single infectious agent. It kills nearly two million people each year; in 2013, 9 million people fell ill with TB and 1.5 million of them died from the disease'. I can't help but wonder how long the TB in me might have remained inactive and undiagnosed, had pregnancy not weakened my immune system when it did. There's no telling how much more damage it might have caused me. This is why I remain grateful that Edwin got his visa when he did!

Although it is difficult, if not impossible, for anyone to do much about a weakened immune system when pregnant or suffering from a major illness such as HIV, medical experts still advise that people do all they can to maintain a healthy diet and live in a clean environment to help strengthen their immune system and keep TB at bay.

The occurrence of spinal TB is minimal, especially in pregnant women, and this could be because truly there are few people who have the disease or that people who have it just don't realise it. During my visit to the nursing manager at the chest clinic, I was told that in the last five years in Birmingham and Solihull alone, they have seen and treated 101 patients with TB located in places outside the lungs—that is, in the bones and joints. While from this statistic it is not clear how many had ST, one could infer that the number of ST patients might be few.

The whole ordeal was most definitely unpleasant. My life seemed torn apart, not being able to walk at all and at the same time unable to be a real mum to my new baby. Today I am left with a few scars, such as the stiffness and odd pains due to the mechanical changes in my back and off-and-on heaviness on my left ribcage. However, after many years, I would say that amidst these challenges I am doing well. Years ago my physio advised me to rest whenever I have pains in my back so as to relieve the muscles, and if the pains go, I should know it was a muscular-related pain. So far, this remedy has worked.

The list of things I can now do is much longer but I miss the things I can't do. I miss not being able to do what I refer to as my own acrobatics: raising my arms above my head with my hands interlocked and bringing them over my head in a clockwise swing to the front. Additionally, I would have loved to be able to play without fear when my boys urge me to take part in a bedtime play which I call 'free fall'—that is, to fall backwards on the bed like a log.

As a teenager, I used to pride myself on being six feet tall and walking upright compared with some of my friends who slouched when they walked. Another scar from the illness is that I now walk slightly bent over due to my further-curved spine. I did not realise this until friends brought it to my notice and this has now made me conscious, so I always try to straighten up even though I believe the harm has already been done. Now that I am slightly shorter than six feet, I feel a bit cheated by nature, but this loss is nothing compared to the fact that I am alive and well, and so is my son.

I initially could not reconcile with having foreign objects in my body, especially during those times when it felt as though the rods or screws were piercing my skin. It is funny how I used to think that if I walked or lie in a certain way they would get adjusted inside. With this discomfort going on for a while, I visited my neurosurgeon in 2011 and asked him to take out the rods. His response the two times I suggested it was the same: he said he would do it only if the pain was overwhelming and causing damage, because he could not guarantee I would have a better back after taking out the rods. After weighing the discomfort against the doctor's response, I chose to live with and embrace my situation, which could have been far worse. To be honest, after seven years, I no longer feel strange with the rods in me.

Battling with this illness and all it presented, plus being separated from my baby at a time when we ought to have been bonding, was surely not the place to be. However, looking back from the time Auntie took us into her home to when I was at the QE with the lovely staff, plus all the kind-hearted people who took care of JD and me, I am certain that throughout this challenging time God planted the right people in my life to help me and my family go through this ordeal much more easily. And as Edwin said, no one is taught how to be a mother or a father; if there were a manual, perhaps it would have made the parenting experience a lot easier. But as there is none, we both parented JD based on what we knew and how much we could do physically. Neither of us was happy to have our son live away from us but it was our belief in Christ, which was all we had, that saw us through each day, knowing that this ordeal was indeed a passing phase.

When my mum said she could not come I was devastated, to say the least. I could not bring myself to tell Auntie or friends the truth as a result. Looking back, I now understand that it was God teaching me to learn to trust Him and Him alone. I now believe that this was why He asked my mother, who I know loves me to bits, not to come to England. Growing up, my siblings and I had always seen our mum as our pillar of strength, to the point that whenever we were ill or had a problem, a phone call to our mum was the cure or solution; and if I am honest, this was always the case, for my mother is a devout and praying woman of God. I again believe God used this painful experience to teach me to focus on Him as my source and solution. How could I not learn to trust God when my son was left to the mercies of strangers? I was forced to trust Him better and He did not fail to prove that He can be trusted, for our dear son Jedidiah has grown into a healthy and lovely young boy. He is independent and confident. And this is why even when I recall my past ordeal I have more than one reason to be grateful. I am grateful to God for my healing, for another lease of life, and for keeping my family safe and intact.

My neurosurgeon gave me two pieces of advice: one was that I should not put strain on my back and the other that I should not get pregnant until eighteen months after surgery to allow my spine to heal properly. We wholly complied with his advice and surpassed it, for our second son was born three years and eight months later. I recall that during my second pregnancy my friends were understandably quite concerned about my back and would always ask if the pregnancy was going well. I personally was stunned by how well I was and more so by how strong my back was. Not that I expected it to crumble or anything of that sort, but as it is a norm for pregnant women to have the odd back pains, I waited each day expecting this and *not once* did I have *any* pain in my back. I actually believe that the metalwork must have given it additional strength, which is why it did not seem to suffer from the baby's weight.

My friends held another baby shower prior to my due date, but this time it involved an awful lot of prayers as they, especially those who knew me during my first pregnancy, prayed fervently, asking that God protect my health and baby's so that everything would go well. Thankfully, the pregnancy went swimmingly well and so did the delivery of our second son in May 2012.

Even if I did cooperate with my doctors and adhered to all medical advice given, I did not realise that I had still not fully come to terms with having been infected with TB, let alone having it in my spine. I got to realise the depth of this denial only when I visited my surgeon in January 2015 to have a discussion with him in order to glean any more information that would help me with writing this book. My neurosurgeon, whom I had not seen for over two years, was very pleased to see me and when he began to talk me through the procedure done on the night of September 22nd 2008, he referred to how badly the TB had affected my spine. Again I jumped in and straightforwardly told him that I did not intend writing about TB so he should kindly stick to explaining the surgical operation. Thinking about this as I caught the train back to work that afternoon made me laugh and snap out of my delusion. *How on earth did I think that I could write my story without including information about its cause?* This event made me realise that I had been living a lie by not fully accepting that I had TB so I immediately decided to make it the last time I lived that lie.

I believe that another reason for not reconciling with the truth early enough is because of the stigma associated with having TB. It sounds quite foolish to me now but back at home, TB was very much likened to HIV, which is surely not something one would happily want to be associated with nor make public knowledge. Today, and this very minute as I write this book, I can no longer be bothered about what stigma or shame is linked to it; instead, I am glad and grateful for knowing what I know today. With the relatively sparse amount of comprehensive knowledge on Spinal Tuberculosis that exists today, I have chosen to tell my story so that people can be educated and that it will hopefully, help to save a life and perhaps prevent another child from missing out on the love of the mother.

It is true that a lot happened to me and to my family as a result of this mysterious illness; nonetheless, one sure thing that comes out of it is how many positive remarks people make when they see me. Every so often, when I tell people my story or when I see someone who knew me when I was ill, they always seem amazed to see how well I now look and how *vertical* I am!

I hear comments like "you have done really well, Esosa," or "you look amazing; I can't believe this is you!"

"Wow! Glory to God for how far you have come!" I hear them say.

Upon hearing this, I tell them that all of who I am today is a result of God's grace, for I know I could not have come through without it. And as was said by JD in my dream, "All men will see the glory of God and give Him thanks."

I do not know how or when I contracted TB in the first place, nor can I decipher why the complete report by the radiographer was ignored, but I choose to live by these words:

You can decide to remain a victim by dwelling on how things should have been or use the experience to grow stronger and wiser. ~ Bob Gass

I choose the latter!

Gallery

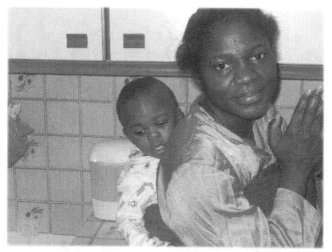

Me with JD on my back in our lakeside flat in 2009.

Me and Edwin on our wedding day.

Me while working in Abuja city, 2003.

Me at about 5months pregnant, out with
Edwin at the park near our house.

Me and my mum when she visited me
in Newcastle in March 2004.

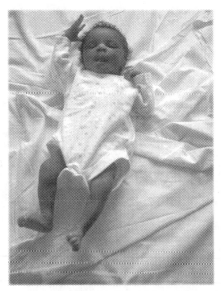

JD, a few days old in Good Hope hospital.

In front of Fothergill Maternity ward on the day
of discharge from Good Hope hospital.

JD's naming ceremony day.

Edwin with JD, a few days after we got
home from Good Hope hospital

Me with JD when Ada brought him to visit me at the QE.

Me with JD.

Me and JD during one of our visits to the
chest clinic at Good Hope hospital.

Me and JD out on a walk at the park by our
house during my months of rehabilitation.

Me and JD at Bose's house when she helped to baby-
sit him shortly after I resumed work in June 2009

JD with Bose during his dedication in July 2009.

Me and my sister, Itohan when she visited in October 2009.

JD and his brother, Jonathan.

Bibliography

Badve S.A. et al, 2011. Tuberculosis of spine with neurological deficit in advanced pregnancy: a report of three cases. *United States National Library of Medicine.* 11(1), 9-16.

Dass B., Puet T.A., Watanakunakorn C., 2002. Tuberculosis of the spine (Pott's disease) presenting as compression fractures. *Journal of the International Spinal Cord Society.* 40 (11), 604-608.

Garg R.K. and Somvanshi D.S., 2011. Spinal tuberculosis: A review. *The Journal of Spinal Cord Medicine* [online], Maney. 34(5), 440-454.

Jain S., (2014). Keeping spinal tuberculosis at bay. *The Hindu Newspaper* [online], 6 August 2014. Available from:

http://www.thehindu.com/features/metroplus/fitness/keeping-spinal-tuberculosis-at-bay/article6287496.ece

[Accessed 10 May 2015].

Mbata G. C.,Ofondu E., Ajuonuma B., Asodike V. C., and Chukwumam D., 2012. Tuberculosis of the spine (Pott's disease) presenting as hemiparesis: Case Report. *African Journal of Respiratory Medicine.* 8(1), 18-20.

Safo S. and Lieberman G., 2009 Pott's Disease: A Radiological Review of Tuberculous Spondylitis.

Tuberculosis: Fact sheet (2015). World Health Organisation [online]. Available from:

http://www.who.int/mediacentre/factsheets/fs104/en/

[Accessed 10 June 2015].

Easmon C., (2013) Tuberculosis: a Review

http://www.netdoctor.co.uk/diseases/facts/tuberculosis.htm#ixzz3ieBYgWc8

[Accessed 13 August 2015].

Other Sources

Birmingham and Solihull Tuberculosis Clinic.

Home Office, Immigration and Nationality Directorate. Section 54 of the Nationality, Immigration and Asylum Act 2002. Local authority briefing pack.

Bone Spine online database.

Centres for Disease Control and Prevention online database.

National Institute for Health and Care Excellence (NICE) online database.

Sattvik Spine Foundation online database.

The Journal of Bone and Joint Surgery.

United Kingdom National Health Service database.

United States of America, National Center for Biotechnology Information and National Library of Medicine.

Printed in the United States
By Bookmasters